READING HEBREW BIBLE NARRATIVES

ESSENTIALS OF BIBLICAL STUDIES

Series Editor

Patricia K. Tull, Louisville Presbyterian Theological Seminary

READING HEBREW BIBLE NARRATIVES
J. Andrew Dearman

THE HISTORY OF BRONZE AND IRON AGE ISRAEL
Victor H. Matthews

NEW TESTAMENT CHRISTIANITY IN THE ROMAN WORLD
Harry O. Maier

WOMEN IN THE NEW TESTAMENT WORLD
Susan E. Hylen

Reading Hebrew
Bible Narratives

J. ANDREW DEARMAN

OXFORD
UNIVERSITY PRESS

OXFORD
UNIVERSITY PRESS

Oxford University Press is a department of the University of Oxford. It furthers
the University's objective of excellence in research, scholarship, and education
by publishing worldwide. Oxford is a registered trade mark of Oxford University
Press in the UK and certain other countries.

Published in the United States of America by Oxford University Press
198 Madison Avenue, New York, NY 10016, United States of America.

© Oxford University Press 2019

Library of Congress Cataloging-in-Publication Data
Names: Dearman, J. Andrew (John Andrew), 1951– author.
Title: Reading Hebrew Bible narratives / By J. Andrew Dearman.
Description: New York, NY : Oxford University Press, [2019] |
Includes bibliographical references and index.
Identifiers: LCCN 2018013404 (print) | LCCN 2018016705 (ebook) |
ISBN 9780190246501 (updf) | ISBN 9780190246518 (epub) |
ISBN 9780190246488 (hardcover) | ISBN 9780190246495 (pbk.) |
ISBN 9780190246525 (online content)
Subjects: LCSH: Bible as literature. | Bible—Criticism, Narrative.
Classification: LCC BS535 (ebook) | LCC BS535 .D43 2019 (print) |
DDC 221.6/6—dc23
LC record available at https://lccn.loc.gov/2018013404

1 3 5 7 9 8 6 4 2

Paperback printed by Webcom, Inc., Canada
Hardback printed by Bridgeport National Bindery, Inc., United States of America

CONTENTS

SECTION II THE WORLD BEHIND THE TEXT

SECTION III THE WORLDS OF
AND BEHIND THE TEXT

SECTION IV THE WORLD IN FRONT
OF THE TEXT

SERIES INTRODUCTION

The past three decades have seen an explosion of approaches to study of the Bible, as older exegetical methods have been joined by a variety of literary, anthropological, and social models. Interfaith collaboration has helped change the field, and the advent of more cultural diversity among biblical scholars in the west and around the world has broadened our reading and interpretation of the Bible. These changes have also fueled interest in Scripture's past: both the ancient Near Eastern and Mediterranean worlds out of which Scripture came and the millennia of premodern interpretation through which it traveled to our day. The explosion of information and perspectives is so vast that no one textbook can any longer address the many needs of seminaries and colleges where the Bible is studied.

In addition to these developments in the field itself are changes in the students. Traditionally the domain of seminaries, graduate schools, and college and university religion classes, now biblical study also takes place in a host of alternative venues. As lay leadership in local churches develops, nontraditional, weekend, and online preparatory classes have mushroomed. As seminaries in Africa, Asia, and Latin America grow, particular need for inexpensive, easily available materials is clear. As religious controversies over the Bible's origins and norms continue to dominate the airwaves, congregation members and even curious nonreligious folk seek reliable paths into particular topics. And teachers themselves continue to seek guidance in areas of the ever-expanding field of scriptural study with which they may be less than familiar.

A third wave of changes also makes this series timely: shifts in the publishing industry itself. Technologies and knowledge are shifting so rapidly that large books are out of date almost before they are in print. The internet and the growing popularity of e-books call for flexibility and accessibility in marketing and sales. If the days when one expert can sum up the field in a textbook are gone, also gone are the days when large, expensive multi-authored tomes are attractive to students, teachers, and other readers.

During my own years of seminary teaching, I have tried to find just the right book or books for just the right price, at just the right reading level for my students, with just enough information to orient them without drowning them in excess reading. For all the reasons stated above, this search was all too often less than successful. So I was excited to be asked to help Oxford University Press assemble a select crew of leading scholars to create a series that would respond to such classroom challenges. Essentials of Biblical Studies comprises freestanding, relatively brief, accessibly written books that provide orientation to the Bible's contents, its ancient contexts, its interpretive methods and history, and its themes and figures. Rather than a one-size-had-better-fit-all approach, these books may be mixed and matched to suit the objectives of a variety of classroom venues as well as the needs of individuals wishing to find their way into unfamiliar topics.

I am confident that our book authors will join me in returning enthusiastic thanks to the editorial staff at Oxford University Press for their support and guidance, especially Theo Calderara, who shepherded the project in its early days, and Dr. Steve Wiggins, who has been a most wise and steady partner in this work since joining OUP in 2013.

Patricia K. Tull
Series Editor

READING HEBREW BIBLE NARRATIVES

Introduction

The text is a vehicle of representation. Literature is a verbal reconstruction of a world, analogous to the visual representation of the world in art. It may represent the real world (in which case it may appear historical even when it is not), or a non-real world. A literary interpretation of the Bible probes the Bible's construction of the world and analyzes the forms of expression through which that world is constructed.

—ADELE BERLIN[1]

BROADLY DEFINED, A NARRATIVE IS an account of connected events provided by a writer or speaker. The Hebrew Bible (HB) has many such narratives among its collection of books, whose composition spanned a period of centuries from oral tradition to completed form (ca. 1200–100 BCE). They are historical narratives in the sense defined here; they render the past not only by constructing that world for readers but also in interpreting a remembered history for them. In brief, they explain the past for Israelite readers, and in doing so, they seek to persuade their readers of the significance of the portrayal for the ongoing religious identity of Israel. Such "persuasive explaining" has made them religious classics. Readers of an introductory phrase such as "it happened late in the afternoon, when David got up from his rest" (2 Sam. 11:2) or "on that night the king could not sleep" (Esther 6:1) anticipate an interesting account to follow! Narratives in the HB entertain, even as they explain and persuade on the great subjects of God, the world, and the human condition.

In the HB, the specific events of a narrative, short or long in length, also presuppose a larger storyline—namely, the remembered history of ancient Israel and the world from which it emerged. For example, a short story (the book of Ruth) begins "in the days when the judges judged" and the longer narrative in the book of 1 Samuel begins with the notice that a man from Ramathaim in the hill country of Ephraim used to go yearly to worship the Lord at the shrine in Shiloh (1 Sam. 1:1–3). Both the presenter and the intended audience will have some connection to a previous period (called the "Judges") and recognition of the tribal area of Ephraim, along with a place of worship in the town of Shiloh. As we shall see, the events from the time of the Judges presented in Ruth connect with prior generations of people from the tribe of Judah (Ruth 4:11–12), as well as to central characters in the monarchical history of Israel that followed the era of the Judges (4:18–22). In the case of the man from Ramathaim in 1 Samuel 1, he turns out to be the father of Samuel, a pivotal figure during the period of the Judges who figured prominently in Israel's transition to monarchy.

Connections between events in narratives obviously depend on the author presenting them, even as readers evaluate and respond from their own perspectives. An author of a story and a narrator may be the same person, but not necessarily so, since a narrator can be a character or a voice in an account. Authors (presenters) in the HB are not disinterested parties. They adopt and adapt earlier materials, which may well constrain the way they render matters; they compare and contrast what they have received, as well as create accounts based on their own experiences. Inevitably, the interests and commitments of presenters drive selectivity in their presentation. Even if their goal is a faithful rendition of what they received, they interpret data as they assimilate and represent them.

Narratives in the HB are a form of storytelling, a universal human phenomenon. And they come in more than one literary form. Books like Ruth and 1 Samuel are recognized examples of a narrative text, mostly in prose. The book of Job is mostly in poetry, but it presents a narrative to readers through its introduction and conclusion. Narratives are the most common type of literature in the HB, central to the way that ancient Israel and its heirs render an account of themselves.

It is worth a moment's reflection to consider the "narrativity" of the HB historically and culturally by way of select examples from antiquity. After all, the HB is but one collection of a rich inheritance from ancient Near Eastern and Mediterranean civilizations. For Western civilization, the impact of the Bible and classical texts from Greco-Roman society has been immense. This means, among other things, that such texts also have a long history of interpretation associated with them. Take, for example, *The Iliad*, an epic poem from Archaic Greece, which presents a story about warfare among city-states, the exploits of heroes, and the influence of the Olympian deities in human affairs. It is basic to the understanding of the larger classical and Hellenistic civilizations, a centerpiece of their literary canon. An approximate date of 750 BCE is plausible, with most scholars concluding that the author drew upon a variety of older traditions reaching back into the Late Bronze and Late Mycenaean periods, even as they were shaped for re-presentation in light of later concerns. Correspondingly, the Pentateuch (Torah) in the HB, although different in terms of literary form from *The Iliad*, is central to Judaism's self-understanding. It, too, draws upon a variety of older traditions that were shaped for re-presentation in light of later concerns.

The Greek playwright Aeschylus (ca. 525–456 BCE) wrote dramas presenting tragic narratives, like *Seven Against Thebes*, with its poignant story of two brothers and rivals for the throne of the city-state of Thebes. While readers may be impressed with the "entertainment factor" in the play, an important element to the modern West, a Greek tragedy offered powerful portrayals of human nature in story and dialogue. While not a play, the book of Job contains powerful dialogues in story form on how humans respond to suffering and grapple with God's involvement in it.

The Greek historian Herodotus (ca. 484–425 BCE) compiled a prose work entitled *The Histories*, which recounts and explains the origins of conflict between the Persian Empire and certain Greek city-states, while making observations about any number of topics. Interpreters have called him the "father of history"[2] for the manner in which he narrates the relationships between rival civilizations and their leaders, and his manner of rendering a cultural identity of his own culture. In the HB, several of the larger narrative books similarly present accounts of Israelite national history and self-understanding.

Of these three works from ancient Greece, a modern reader might conclude that *The Histories* is the most obvious narrative in form, but Homer's epic and Aeschylus's tragedies also present stories in poetry and dialogue. As noted, with Aeschylus's works, the performative element is obvious, whereby an audience hears and responds in various ways, but one can say that narratives, too, are artistic presentations and intend to engage hearers and readers.

The Ancient Near East (ANE), the first cultural home of the HB, produced narratives that represent the self-understanding of the peoples who inhabited it. The *Gilgamesh Epic* emerged early in Mesopotamian culture (third millennium BCE) and continued to develop over a period of centuries as it found a prominent place in the civilizations of the Fertile Crescent. Readers of it and the biblical book of Genesis will see common motifs, such as the power of a flood to erase human life, the survival of a human figure, and the futile search for eternal life. Mesopotamia also produced several poems that explore the human condition in light of suffering and death. It is a universal dilemma explored through different literary forms in different cultures. The Mesopotamian poems are not narratives per se, but like a Greek tragedy or the book of Job, they do render a portrait of the mysterious relationship between humanity and the divine world.

From ancient Ugarit, a Bronze Age city on the coast of northern Syria, comes an epic of the life of a king named Kirta and his struggles to maintain his family and life. Indeed, narratives about royalty, their exploits and their piety (or lack thereof), are common in antiquity, since monarchs influence much of the corporate life around them. From Iron Age II (ca. 900–550 BCE), a number of royal annals from the Neo-Assyrians and Neo-Babylonian kings have survived. They are primary sources for scholars in reconstructing the history of the Assyrian and Babylonian Empires, even as readers encounter the worldview and self-understanding of the presenters in these accounts. Similarly, kingship is a major theme in the biblical books of Samuel, Kings, and Chronicles.

The three works from classical antiquity cited here are characteristic of ancient Greek civilization, just as those cited from the ANE are characteristic of Semitic cultures. They are characteristic in two related senses: In the first instance, they were literary treasures of their respective cultures. In the second sense, they are what later readers encounter as standard texts of a culture. We can say, therefore, that they constitute part of the literary canon of classical Greek civilization or that of the ANE.

The HB, analogously, consists of writings that are classics first for Jewish civilization and then, in translation, for Christian cultures, where these writings came to be known as the Old Testament (OT). The HB/OT is "canonical" as well in a specifically religious sense, in that the HB is the sacred Scriptures of Judaism and (in related forms) the OT is the first testament of the Christian Bible. And if that were not enough of a historic footprint in world literature, the HB/OT influenced the Quran, the sacred text of Islam. The narratives in the HB, therefore, are classics in more than one sense of that term, with a rich history of interpretation associated with them.

THREE CATEGORIES FOR A CLOSE READING OF NARRATIVES IN THE HB/OT

A current model of biblical interpretation arranges questions and approaches in three categories: the world of the text, the world behind the text, and the world in front of the text. We will use these categories in what follows. We begin with the world of the text. Our subject matter is a literary text and thus we begin by examining its literary/communicative properties. Chapters 2 through 6 are concerned primarily with the world of the text represented in the narratives under exploration, which we will look at from various angles (facets, as in a cut diamond). We will, however, note some connections with the other two categories as we proceed. Subsequent chapters examine historical and cultural contexts in the world behind the narratives. Chapters 7 and 8 are concerned primarily with these matters and their influences on the narratives. Chapters 9 and 10 will look at two accounts, building on methods accumulated in previous chapters. Our explorations will also lead us to matters related to the world in front of the text—that is, the historical-cultural context of readers ancient and modern, and how that context influences the reading of biblical narratives. Chapter 11 explores aspects of this phenomena in what we call "reception history."

Beginning in chapter 2, all subsequent chapters engage biblical narratives directly. We will offer methodological comments as we proceed. And some narratives we will look at repeatedly, engaging them variously in different chapters. This is not a text on hermeneutical theory. Instructors who use this textbook can provide that dimension better than the author.[3]

WHY CHOOSE THE BIBLICAL NARRATIVES EXAMINED IN THIS WORK?

There are two purposes at work in selecting the biblical narratives under examination. The first is simply to have a range of narratives with which to engage. Hence, we will look at some accounts in Genesis, Judges, Ruth, 2 Samuel, 1 Kings, Ezra, and Nehemiah. Several of these narratives share the common social institution of the human family. They assist with a second purpose. We will look at multiple accounts that deal with matters of family, marriage, and the birth of children, returning periodically to them in different chapters. In this way, we will see how these subjects are dealt with by different authors and how those accounts might assist us in identifying broader characteristics of biblical narratives.

TWO ANALOGIES FOR CONSIDERATION

Narratives in the HB are like cut diamonds. Gemstone technicians—they are really artists—cut facets (flat surfaces) to shape a diamond into a jewel. A cut diamond will have multiple facets, and one cannot "see" all there is to it from a single vantage point. Each facet provides an angle of vision to see something of the jewel's brilliance. Methods to examine texts are like looking at different facets to appreciate and evaluate a diamond's properties. Few people, furthermore, appreciate a raw diamond. It is the shaped stone for presentation that engages a viewer, just as it is the author who shapes a narrative and thus exposes the brilliance for readers.

The second analogy comes from observing the lives of twin grandsons. Think jewels of a different kind! Family members typically note how different they are, even when they are engaged in the same activities. Nonfamily members often remark on how similar they are. Of course, family members talk about their similarities and nonfamily members observe their differences—and we should be quick to point out that there is no suggestion of right or wrong in either approach. In the academic study of biblical narratives, there is typically an emphasis on the singularity/uniqueness of a given account. What, for example, makes Job's combination of story and dialogue unique? Several things! On the one hand, there is nothing quite like it elsewhere in the HB/OT or in the surviving literature of the ANE, although human suffering is a perennial topic in the world's literature. On the other hand, as part of Israel's canonical collection, Job is one member of a literary family (so to speak). Its comparison with "siblings" may indicate something of its uniqueness, but it will also highlight the ways in which the book commonly addresses the topic of God and the human condition. We will be asking both kinds of questions about the narratives under examination, seeking what is unique about any one of them, as well as their similarity to other texts.

1

Narratives in
the Hebrew Bible

THE NARRATIVE PORTIONS OF THE Hebrew Bible are spread throughout its three major sections, which in Jewish tradition are The Pentateuch (Torah), The Prophets, and the Writings. The Christian Old Testament contains all the books of the Hebrew Bible, as well as some additional ones known collectively as the Apocrypha. This latter collection varies in content, depending on whether it is the collection of the Roman Catholic Church or one from the communion of churches known as Orthodoxy. The Protestant Old Testament contains the same books as the Hebrew Bible, but they are typically arranged in a different order.

Here are thumbnail sketches of the books and/or collections of books. These do not exhaust the narrative materials in the Hebrew Bible, but they provide a quick orientation to the majority of them.

The **Pentateuch**, also known as The Torah or The Law, comprises the five books of Genesis, Exodus, Leviticus, Numbers, and Deuteronomy. They present an account of the creation of the world and its human families (Gen. 1–11), followed by four generations of the family of Abraham and Sarah (Gen. 12–50), whose descendants become slaves in Egypt (Exod. 1–15). They constitute themselves in twelve tribes named for Israel, one of their ancestors. Once freed from slavery by the power of their God, they receive instructions from God at the Mountain of Sinai (Exod. 20–Num. 10:10). After nearly forty years of wandering in the wilderness between Egypt and the land of Canaan (Num. 10:11–21:35), the tribes are camped east of the Jordan River, where they receive additional instructions from God through their leader Moses, who then dies before the tribes begin their occupation of Canaan (Num. 22–Deut. 34). The Pentateuch has a narrative frame and structure, even as it presents its story in various literary forms.

The **Former Prophets** (a Jewish term) comprise the six books of Joshua, Judges, 1–2 Samuel, and 1–2 Kings. The Old Testament does not have a collective term for these books. Together they present the history of the Israelite tribes as they occupy the land of Canaan (Josh. 1–12), divide the land into tribal inheritances (Josh. 13–19), establish themselves during periods of conflict with neighbors (Judges), and finally emerge as a monarchical state (1–2 Samuel, 1 Kings 1–11). Civil and religious disputes will lead to the formation of two monarchical states, one keeping the name of Israel and the other using a tribal name, Judah. Eventually Israel comes to a political end at the hands of the Assyrians and then Judah comes to a political end at the hands of the Babylonians (1 Kings 12–2 Kings 25). Modern interpreters sometimes speak of these books plus Deuteronomy as the Deuteronomistic History (DtrH). This is because of vocabulary and themes held in common between them.

1 and 2 Chronicles is a selective retelling of the history of Israel and Judah that draws on the Pentateuch, but more frequently on traditions held in common with 1 and 2 Samuel and 1–2 Kings. The storyline that it renders continues past the defeat of Judah and Jerusalem at the hands of the Babylonians to the time when King Cyrus of Persia allows the return of exiles to Jerusalem and Judah for rebuilding projects.

Ezra and **Nehemiah** present the resettlement of Judah and Jerusalem during the period of the Persian Empire. The figure of Ezra, a Jewish priest from Babylon, is common to both books.

Esther recounts a time of threat to the Jewish communities in the Persian Empire and the work of two Jews, Esther and Mordecai, to mitigate the threat.

Jonah is an account of an Israelite prophet who goes to Nineveh, the capital of the Assyrian Empire, to deliver a divine message.

Ruth is the story of a Moabite woman who marries into a Judahite family and becomes the great grandmother of King David.

Job rehearses briefly the misfortune of a pious man and presents various dialogues between Job's friends and between Job and God.

Daniel has a cycle of stories about three Hebrew exiles in Babylon, the most prominent of whom is named Daniel.

There are several observations one can make about the foregoing thumbnail sketches. The first is how colorless, indeed dull, they are! As quick summaries, they don't do justice to the drama of the biblical narratives. A modern reader likely finds tedious the list of pre-flood generations in Genesis 5 or nine chapters of genealogies in 1 Chronicles. But accounts like the near sacrifice of Abraham's son (Gen. 22), the crossing of the Red Sea (Exod. 14–15), the prophet Elijah's contest on Mt. Carmel (1 Kings 18), or Daniel's night in a den of lions (Dan. 6:10–28) have gripped readers for centuries. Explanation and persuasion, along with entertaining literary artistry, make for engaging presentations.

Second, the list is not complete. For example, the writing prophets may have narrative accounts along with poetic speeches. The most prominent example is the book of Jeremiah. A minor prophet like Amos preserves just one biographical passage (7:10–17) among its prophetic speeches. Several of them preserve none. As noted here, the minor prophet Jonah is a narrative presentation; essentially it is a short story like the books of Ruth and Esther and not a collection of prophetic oracles. All considered, narratives make up the largest portion of the HB.

Third, we need to keep in mind some basic literary distinctions. We are using a broad definition of narrative, like the modern term "story" we noted earlier, a definition that is capable of encompassing several more specific genres. Literary analysts can identify a narrative more precisely as a myth, a fable, a legend, a biographical account, historical report, an etiology, or an epic. Moreover, a narrative presentation itself may contain a variety of genres. For example, the book of Exodus contains a dramatic narrative, moving initially from the predicament of Israelite slaves in Egypt to a conclusion at Mt. Sinai, with the construction of a tent to represent divine presence among them. Yet it includes a song of victory to commemorate the crossing of the Red Sea (Exod. 15:1–21), similar in form to a hymn in the book of Psalms, as well as a collection of instructions in Exodus 21:1–23:19, similar in form to an ancient law code. Exodus thus tells a story with multiple literary forms.

A book may be largely devoid of narrative text, but connected nevertheless to a narrative it provides. We mentioned earlier the book of Job as an example. It begins with two brief chapters that set the stage, as it were, for rounds of poetic dialogue between various characters, comprising some 90 percent of the book. It concludes even more briefly with a prose report (Job 42:7–17). The dialogues would be interpreted differently if the narrative "bookends" were missing.

Fourth, in reading the historical narratives in the HB, we are dealing first with literature. This seems such a facile statement, but it is a reminder that our primary questions and approach are for literary exploration rather than historical reconstruction. Texts, narrative and otherwise, may contain data relevant for historical and social-cultural reconstruction, but in terms of method, we examine first their communicative functions, which we have proposed are broadly that of explanation and persuasion. As noted in the introduction, it is the way they render the world (analogously to a painting) that is of first interest, although we will have occasions in what follows to ask about both historical reconstruction and cultural context. After all, the historical narratives of the HB are primary sources for the history of ancient Israel, and they can be analyzed in the context of other sources (e.g., archeological) from the ANE in reconstructing that history.

Let's briefly examine Joshua 1–12 to show the distinction between reading for historical reconstruction and interpreting as literature. The narrative presents a successful conquest of Canaan by the united twelve tribes of Israel under the leadership of Joshua. This succinctly summarizes the account. Scholars offer a variety of responses to these chapters as windows onto the history of Israel in the latter half of the second millennium BCE. Indeed, there is a long history of discussion among interpreters regarding the historical setting and reliability of the narratives. It is a standard topic in introductions to the HB. How united were the tribes in the Late Bronze Age? Were all the Canaanite cities mentioned actually inhabited at the time? These are some of the questions of historical-cultural context in the world behind the text. Although intriguing questions, the narratives of Joshua 1–12 tell little about military strategy or chronology and were likely compiled centuries after the period they portray.

In terms of plot and theme (concepts that will we describe later), they explain how Israel occupied its ancestral home as the result of divine guidance and aid. The explanation here should be compared to the portrait in the book of Judges that follows, where individual tribes already in Canaan are not united in a single confederation and face difficulties with numerous other inhabitants of the land before the rise of monarchy in Israel. Comparison with other data in the HB is thus one way to approach the question of historical reconstruction. Archeologists and historians have data on the settlement patterns in Canaan of the Late Bronze Age. That data, such as excavation reports on the cities of Jericho and Hazor, provide another avenue of approach. Moreover, there are contemporary literary sources from the ANE (e.g., Amarna Tablets, Merneptah Stele) with which to compare and contrast the biblical texts. The intersection of a close examination of the Joshua narratives and possible historical-cultural contexts behind them offers stimulating reading of them.

The narratives themselves describe events in a theologically straightforward manner. Israel is successful in battle because God gives them victory. They succeed when ritually prepared and in compliance with divine instruction. They are unsuccessful when disobedient to divine command and God gives them over to their opponents. Such a portrait explains to later readers how their ancestors came to a land of promise, and it seeks to persuade later readers that they, too, should be obedient to divine command. The question is not whether historical data can be derived from it but, rather, what kind of data, given the theme of the conquest narratives and what historians can reconstruct of the era from other sources.

Something similar can be said of the annals of King Shalmaneser III of Assyria (ruled 859–824 BCE), even though they were compiled in his lifetime and describe his military exploits in some detail. They are prime sources to reconstruct the history of the Assyrian Empire. And they can be compared to the archeological and textual data from Phoenicia and Syria in the Iron Age. Even so, historical method may not be usable to judge the accuracy of battle details or whether much of a battle took place at all. The annals are also self-serving testimonies to Shalmaneser, depicted as a chosen vessel of the Assyrian deities, and to the splendor of the army, which overwhelms hapless opponents. A prominent theme of the annals is that Assyrian deities intend the expansion of Assyrian rule and that resistance to it is futile; the details of military conquest serve as explanation of this theme.[1]

SOME CONCEPTS FOR READING NARRATIVES IN THE HB/OT

A secondary teacher once referred to the five "W questions" as a way to teach reading comprehension. She said that asking "Who," "What," "Where," "When," and "Why" of a story provides ways to interact with it and to explore its meaning. The terms that follow are more typically used by practitioners of narrative analysis, but the five basic questions find a place among them.

Plot

If a narrative is an account of connected events, the plot is that which connects the events through a beginning, a continuation, and a conclusion. To use a building metaphor, it is the architecture of a story. Often a narrative has dilemma or conflict that comes to some resolution. Defining the dilemma or conflict in a narrative can put the plot into sharper relief, along with the way(s) a conclusion to it is reached. Discerning a plot in a story can involve all five questions, but the "What is the story about?" and "Why is it told?" are central to it.

We may first think of the plot as applicable to a longer narrative or a complete book, but a plot is inherent to virtually any story in the HB. Interpreters may explore the plots of books like Genesis and 1 Samuel or, say, one of the stories in them. We will look at both types of approach in what follows. Starting with an account from a larger narrative is an easier approach, but charting the plot of a book is also important for reading comprehension.

Analyzing the plot for books like Genesis and 1 Samuel, moreover, is analogous to looking at multiple, intersecting routes on a large road map. There are plot lines in the books themselves and the books can be linked to others in the collective enterprise of Israel's national storyline. Take the book of Genesis, itself a composite work: It includes inherited traditions in it with intriguing plots like the cycle of stories about Abraham and Sarah (chapters 12–25) and Joseph (chapters 37, 39–50). They, in turn, contribute to the plotline of the book. Genesis, moreover, is also the first of five books in the Torah and its narratives play a role in defining the plot of the latter entity.

In the case of 1 Samuel, its narrative continues directly in 2 Samuel. One can explore the plot of 1 and 2 Samuel, as well as that of either book or a portion thereof. But that is not all of the intersecting plot lines to consider. The books of Joshua, Judges, Samuel, and Kings (i.e., the Former Prophets) have been passed down together for centuries to present a connected narrative of Israel's history from occupation of the Promised Land to its loss centuries later at the hands of the Babylonians. At one level of interpretation, their connectedness is an editorial decision. A later community put them together as parts of a larger whole in presenting the storyline of ancient Israel. They are part of a literary and a theological canon. Doubtless there were several hands at work in the composition of these books, but as books they have a certain "family resemblance." As noted earlier, this has prompted modern scholars to see them as connected narratives and to describe them as a DtrH. So it is common in recent decades for interpreters to refer to the six books of Joshua–2 Kings, or to these six plus Deuteronomy, as the DtrH and to investigate themes and vocabulary they have in common. The point at hand is not to argue for the validity of the DtrH as a single narrative but, rather, to reiterate that in exploring the plot of books in the HB, we need to consider how a narrative communicates on its own, as well as how it is configured as part of larger texts in the scriptural canons of Judaism and Christianity.

One more example: On an even larger scale, interpreters refer to the **Primary History** of ancient Israel. They mean by that term the Pentateuch and the Former Prophets—eleven books total. They do not see them as the work of a single writer, but they recognize that in putting the Torah and the Prophets together in a canonical collection, Jews and Christians can read them as a connected story.

Narratives have one or more **Themes**. A theme can be a main idea and/or a recurring subject in a narrative and, as such, is related to a plot. In exploring the question, "What is a story about?" one can cite the central events that constitute it (plot) while using them to discern the main idea(s) driving their presentation. Discerning a theme is one way to answer the question "Why is this story told?" We suggested a couple examples of a theme in the quick descriptions of Joshua 1–12 and Shalmaneser's annals.

Character

A character—an actor in the narrative—may be a simple figure or a more complex one as a story unfolds. Some interpreters refer to simple characters as flat and those that are more complex as round. The terminology is less important than thinking of character portrayal on a scale of developed roles and nuanced traits. "Who are the actors in the story?" should lead directly to the questions "What do they do and what do they contribute to the account?"

Two common elements in the portrayal of characters in the HB are speech and action. Much of what is written about a character consists of direct speech. Think, for example, of the way the book of Genesis begins. God brings the world into ordered existence by speaking. It is difficult to overemphasize this manner of representing biblical characters, divine or human, so pervasive is speech in their narrative portrayal. One effective way of interpreting a biblical story is to mark carefully who is speaking and to whom the character is speaking. In terms of outlining a story (a good habit for discerning plot in a manageable narrative), the speaking roles are often the major elements in it.

Second to speech is action. We might summarize by saying that in the HB, characters are what they do and what they say. Such a description is thrown into sharper relief by the reticence among narrators to describe characters in other ways. Modern storytelling delights in such things as physical descriptions, psychological profiling, and indications of predilections in rounding out its characters. Psychological categories are particularly influential for modern Western readers. So and so, for example, might be presented as tall and nervous, a committed libertarian with a germ phobia, and attachment issues. Descriptions of characters' hearts and minds can be part of a narrative portrayal in the HB, but they take a back seat to speech and actions. Without accompanying character descriptions, readers infer judgments about them based on what they say and do.

In asking the question, "What does a character do?" we are also asking "Why do they do it?" There are, of course, ways in which narrators answer these questions directly or indirectly in portraying biblical characters. The preceding description suggests that a primary way to answer the "why" question comes in the readers' assessment of reported speech and deeds.

Point of View

Generally speaking, a point of view in a narrative presentation functions like a frame for a picture or the lens of a camera. It offers particularity and focus for readers. We can speak of the point of view of the narrator, who emphasizes some things (a type of framing) and passes over others in presentation, just as we can talk of a character's point of view. Simply put, the presenter's point of view decides what we read and how it is presented. There is no such thing as an all-inclusive picture or portrait, and no comprehensive narrative. Some principle of selectivity is always at work in narrative presentation, a trait closely related to point of view. Each of the five basic questions contributes to the identification of point of view in a narrative, with the "What is the story about?" "Where does it take place?" and "When did it occur?" questions illuminating the matter of selectivity.

According to several interpreters, a prominent feature of narrative in the HB is the "omniscience" of the author. More specifically, this means that the author reports confidently what God knows and what God has said regarding the account at hand. This is a recognizable trait in the literature of antiquity—Homer knows what Athena thinks and reports it, just as Shalmaneser III (in his annals) knows the decisions of the Assyrian deities and reports them. This is explanation and persuasion at work. The biblical narratives are replete with reports of what God said and has done. And it applies to human characterization as well. In primeval times, for example, the "wickedness" of humankind was great, God was sorry to have made them, corporate judgment is formulated, and yet one person finds favor in

God's sight (Gen. 6:5–8). The massive flood of Noah's day is thus explained authoritatively as judgment upon human wickedness. An author's authoritative portrayals are among the most recognizable traits of biblical narratives.

Style

Closely related to point of view and selectivity is narrative style. In asking the question, "What is being presented?" a reader is also asking "How is it being presented?" We might think of style as an aspect of literary artistry. Modern movies are a good parallel. Think of a good discussion among movie aficionados of the filmmaking style of the Coen brothers (Joel and Ethan), Quentin Tarantino, or Steven Spielberg and how their films reflect directorial style.

Any number of comments might be made about the style of biblical narration when that term is used broadly. One could, for example, cite the preference for direct speech and the omniscience of the narrator as stylistic traits. Two additional traits particularly stand out among HB narratives: terseness and repetition. At first thought, these terms may seem contradictory. It is difficult to be brief (one definition of "terse"), if one repeats data. Terseness in biblical narrative refers to the sparing use of detail in description and the lack of various kinds of background material often provided in other forms of storytelling. We noted earlier, for example, the frequent lack of details in character rendering, apart from speech and action. Think again of the brief formulation of matters leading to the flood of Noah's day (Gen. 6:5–8). It offers a quick summary of primeval times, including what was in the hearts of people and God, in three verses! Terseness also applies to sentence structure, although variation in translation techniques can make this less apparent to modern readers. A Hebrew sentence is typically shorter than those in English, classical Greek, or German.

Repetition in biblical narrative has two primary characteristics. The first relates to individual words and related sounds.
Classical Hebrew of the narratives often repeats words and
sounds, or plays upon them. For example, in Genesis 2:7, the
first human is known as "the man" (*ha'adam*) because he was
made from the "earth" (*adamah*), and in Genesis 3:20, the
first woman is called "Eve" (*hava*), as she was the mother of all
"living" (*hay*).[2] Both wordplays intersect with other references
in the immediate context to the ground and to living creatures.
In the story of Jonah, the verb "go down" (*yarad*) describes
the prophet's trek to a boat (Jon. 1:3, 5) and then to the lower
portion of it, where a similar term describes him as in deep sleep
(*radam*; Jon. 1:5). When swallowed by a great fish, he descends
(Jon. 2:7) even farther to the depths before the fish regurgitates
him and he is brought back up to continue his task.

Readers who do not have facility with the Hebrew language
can be frustrated with repeated references to a Hebrew word or
phrase in the chapters that follow. The reason to cite Hebrew
words or call attention to a wordplay is to help explain how the
narrative says what it says and why certain details may stand
out in the narrative presentation. Wordplay can be difficult to
reproduce in translation. Sometimes a modern translation will
have a footnote pointing out the connection between the two
terms and phrases. The play on *Adam* and *adamah* mentioned
here is a good example. The NRSV rendering of Genesis 2:7
offers the following marginal note: "Or *a man* (Heb. *adam*) of
dust from the ground (Heb. *adamah*)."

Second, there are patterns of larger reiteration and reinforcement, and not just individual words and phrases. The
crossing of the Red Sea (Exod. 14:1–15:21) and the defeat of
the Canaanite general Sisera (Judg. 4–5) have both a prose and
poetic presentation side by side. Individual stories and larger
narratives have patterns of description and implementation, a
related type of repetition. Note in the account of Abraham's

servant in Genesis 24:1-61 how the servant prays for God to manifest steadfast love for Abraham (24:12-13) and later repeats that request in describing its fulfillment (24:26-27, 48-49). The book of Exodus furnishes a good example from a larger narrative: chapters 25-31 present instructions regarding the construction of the tabernacle and its furnishings; Exodus 35-40 then reports in some detail that those instructions are carried out.

SOME BASIC HISTORICAL AND CULTURAL TERMS NEEDED FOR READING BIBLICAL NARRATIVES

In the sketches here regarding the narrative traditions in the HB, we used several terms related to the history and culture of the ANE. What follows are some terms, briefly defined and in basic chronological order, that are basic to the study of the HB:

Middle Bronze Age	ca. 1900–1500 BCE
Late Bronze Age	ca. 1500–1200 BCE
Iron Age I	ca. 1200–950 BCE
Iron Age II	ca. 950–587 BCE

Pre-Monarchic Period. Concludes with the period of Saul, ca. 1050 BCE. In literary terms, it is the period covered in Gen. through 1 Sam. 8.

United Monarchy, ca. 1050–930 BCE. In literary terms, the stories of Saul, David, and Solomon in 1 Sam. 8–1 Kings 11; 1 Chron. 10–2 Chron. 9.

First Temple Period, ca. 965–587 BCE. The period of time of the temple first built by Solomon to its destruction by the Babylonians.

Divided Monarchy, ca. 930–721 BCE. In literary terms, the stories of Israel and Judah as separate states in 1 Kings 12–2 Kings 17; 2 Chron. 10–28.

Assyrian Period, ca. 875–612 BCE. When Assyrian rule expanded westward from its heartland in northern Mesopotamia and encompassed much of the eastern Mediterranean.

Pre-exilic Period. Any portion of Israel and Judah's history before the Babylonian exile, which began in 597 BCE.

Babylonian Period, ca. 605–539 BCE. When Babylonian rule expanded westward from its heartland in southern Mesopotamia and encompassed much of the eastern Mediterranean.

Exile/Exilic Period, ca. 597–538 BCE.

Persian Period, ca. 539–331 BCE. When Persian rule expanded westward from its heartland south of the Caspian Sea and encompassed much of the eastern Mediterranean and Asia Minor. In literary terms, the books of Esther, Ezra, and Nehemiah.

Second Temple Period, ca. 515 BCE–70 CE. The period of time from the rebuilding of the temple in Jerusalem to the destruction of the temple by the Romans.

Post-exilic Period, ca. 538–150 BCE. From the time of Jewish return to Judah and Jerusalem to the end of Hellenistic rule over Jews in their homeland.

Hellenistic Period, ca. 331–150 BCE. From the time of Alexander the Great's conquest of the Middle East until the rise of Jewish independence under the leadership of the Hasmonean family (a.k.a. the Maccabees).

ENTRY POINTS FOR READING
NARRATIVES IN THE HB

We have sketched several points of entry—what we can also call basic methods of approach—for engaging narratives in the HB. We start by examining the literary properties of an account. Those efforts will lead to questions about the world behind the texts, those historical and cultural periods influential on the narrators and their intended audience. We want to be careful listeners and engaged responders to the explanatory and persuading properties of the narratives. As such, we want to think self-consciously about the contexts within which we read—the world in front of the text through which we "see" a biblical narrative.

As noted previously, these basic methods are introductory and illustrated through repetitive engagement with biblical narratives. We are more practice-driven than we are theory-driven. These entry points do not constitute a complete method of interpretation, either. Once readers engage these canonical and classic narratives, there is no end to the questions raised and the avenues to be explored. Remember the analogy of the cut diamond: narratives are multifaceted and should be approached from various vantage points!

We will raise questions along the way that won't get definitive answers. Sometimes the questions are left open-ended and sometimes more than one suggested response is offered. The goal is to encourage an active, responsive reading.

Section I

THE WORLD OF THE TEXT

2

Explanation and Persuasion in Stories of Origins

Two Examples from Genesis

IN WHAT FOLLOWS, WE WILL look at two chapters in the book of Genesis as first exercises in interpreting a biblical narrative. We will offer initial analysis of them as brief narratives on their own and as entry points to the larger narrative of the book of Genesis. We will also come back to these two narratives in subsequent chapters to highlight or reconsider elements in them.

GENESIS 16

If you are generally familiar with the contents of Genesis, please read Genesis 16:1–16 carefully, preferably in two or more translations. If you need a refresher on the book, it is wise to read through it completely before returning to chapter 16. One way to explore a brief account is to construct an outline of it. This simple exercise assists in giving attention to detail and narrative flow. Here is an outline for Genesis 16:

I. Initial problem and action   16:1–3
  A. Sarai's barrenness   16:1a
  B. Hagar as surrogate to acquire a child   16:1b–3

    II. Second problem and action   16:4–6
        A. Hagar conceives with Abram   16:4a
        B. Friction between Sarai and Hagar   16:4b
        C. Friction between Sarai and Abram   16:5–6a
        D. Hagar flees after harsh treatment   16:6b
   III. Angel of the Lord appears to Hagar in
       the wilderness   16:7–12
        A. Angel finds and questions Hagar   16:7–8a
        B. Hagar rehearses her predicament   16:8b
        C. Angel instructs her to return to Sarai   16:9
        D. Angel announces a multitude of descendants   16:10
        E. Angel announces the birth and influence
           of Ishmael   16:11–12
    IV. Hagar's responds by naming the Lord "El Roi"   16:13
     V. Naming the place of encounter with God   16:14
    VI. Birth of Ishmael   16:15
   VII. Chronological notice regarding Abram   16:16

Initial Observations From a Reading of Genesis 16

The outline follows a series of connected events as we explore them for plot and theme. Speech and actions of the characters are the primary building blocks of the account. The first sentence indicates a dilemma, which leads to conflict. Sarai and Abram don't have children. An attempt to have a child through a surrogate (Hagar) causes problems in the household. Readers of Genesis have met Abram and Sarai before and will have a context for the report that they have no children.

The plot develops with the introduction of a new female character named Hagar. She is identified by her ethnicity and by social status as Sarai's slave. The first person to speak is Sarai. She tells her husband that the Lord has prevented her from conceiving and she urges Abram to have sexual relations with Hagar so that "I can have children through her." Modern readers will recognize that older customs of defining family and children are at work here. In typical narrative style, the presenter then reports that what Sarai said comes to pass. Abram and Hagar have sexual relations and she conceives a child.

Hagar's pregnancy leads to tension between Sarai and Hagar. The initial dilemma has taken another form. Sarai complains to Abram about Hagar's response to her. He, in turn, replies that Hagar's status is in her hands. After harsh treatment, Hagar flees. Hagar has neither spoken nor been spoken to in a dramatic sequence of only six verses.

A supernatural figure finds Hagar at a spring in the wilderness. Nothing is said about the physical characteristics of the angel of the Lord. The spring is not an incidental detail (see later). His mysterious identity is somewhat clarified through his speaking as *and* for the Lord, but this duality also complicates readers' perceptions. Everything that we learn about this figure in the account comes from what he says.

In response to a question, Hagar finally speaks, summarizing her predicament in one brief sentence. The angel speaks authoritatively, telling her first to return to her mistress Sarai and then (speaking in the first person voice as the Lord) that he will greatly multiply her offspring—that is, descendants. He provides, furthermore, a birth announcement for her child, names him, and indicates what kind of man he shall be among his relatives. The name Ishmael translates as "God hears." According to the angel, the boy will be called "God hears" because God has "heard" about Hagar's misery.

Hagar responds a second time by giving the angel a name, El Roi, which translates as "God who sees," or perhaps as "God of seeing." This is another wordplay, as she concludes that she remains alive even after seeing God. The narrator then reports on a third name—that of the well where this encounter took place. It is known as Beer-lahai-roi, which can be translated as the "well of the living one who sees me." Here is a third word-play, connecting the name of the well to Hagar's revelatory experience.

Hagar's return to Sarai (and Abram) is assumed, and the account concludes with the report that Hagar bore Abram a son. The boy's name is twice given as Ishmael, along with a comment that Abram was eighty-six years old at his birth.

This outline and summary illustrate several elements previously proposed as characteristic for narratives in the HB. The account has a plot, complete with conflict and a form of resolution, all tersely presented. It contains few reported details regarding the characters other than speech and action. The primary exceptions to this are the description of Ishmael and the concluding comment that Abram was eighty-six years old at Ishmael's birth. Readers may well describe Sarai as angry, frustrated, insecure, and so on, based on her words and deeds, but not because the narrator uses such adjectives. We might think, furthermore, of Hagar as awestruck at the appearance of the angel of the Lord—a plausible deduction from her comment that she remains alive after their encounter—yet no description of the supernatural figure is provided other than authoritative speech. What, we may wonder, does an angel of the Lord look like? Indeed, what do Abram, Sarai, and Hagar look like?

For all its terseness, the account still has repetition for emphasis. There are wordplays on the Hebrew words for "hear" and "see." Three entities receive names in the wordplays: the angel of the Lord, Hagar's son, and the well located between Kadesh and Bered. The second half of the account thus has an etiological function—that is, to provide the origin of names known to the intended audience. Ishmael's name occurs three times in the account, once before he was even born. The concluding statement in verses 15 and 16 repeats basic data, even as a chronological detail is added.

Questions From a Reading of Genesis 16

We noted a couple of questions already; a close literary reading will raise any number of them. A selection of such questions is listed next. It is important to note here that the method of a close literary reading is still an initial approach to a story, not a complete exegetical, cultural, or theological analysis. These questions are chosen, in part, because engaging them will lead readers to employ various methods of investigation to aid in reading comprehension. Rather than attempting a detailed answer to each question, we will use them as illustrations for further approaches to narrative analysis.

1. In comparing translations, what questions stand out for you?
2. How many of the names in the account have a symbolic or representative value?
3. What do we know about Abram and Sarai, and particularly the matter of their childlessness?
4. Are there types of slaves in the ANE, and if so, what kind of slave is Hagar?
5. Is Hagar's ethnicity important to the story or an incidental detail (i.e., she is not from the same people group as Abram and Sarai)?
6. What laws or customs are at work so that the child of Hagar could be considered the child of Abram and Sarai?
7. Why send Hagar back to Sarai?
8. What nation or people group have Ishmael as an ancestor?
9. What is a wild ass and does it characterize Ishmael or the nation that he represents?
10. Who and what is an angel of the Lord?

11. Is there significance to the different terms for deity (Lord, El)?
12. Which, if any, of the characters are sympathetic and is this question important to understanding the account in Genesis 16?

Some of the questions are ways to continue exploring the plot and characters in the account. Other questions also put the account into a larger literary or cultural context. Number 3 is a good example of the latter. As we shall see, the matter of progeny for Abram and Sarai plays a major role in the cycle of stories about them in Genesis and in the larger narrative of Israel's remembered history. Other questions in this category include numbers 2, 8, and 9.

A good example of a question to explore the plot of Genesis 16 is number 6. A practice (slave as surrogate) recognized by earlier readers may well be obscure and/or troublesome to later readers, but it is important nevertheless to the coherence of the account. Other questions in this category include numbers 1, 4, 10, and 11.

Some questions are generated by what interpreters call "reader response." The meaning that readers draw from a story is influenced by their reactions to it. Number 12 is an example of reader response, and it influences how one reads both Genesis 16 and the larger cycle of stories to which it is attached. Aversion to slavery and to mistreatment of women affects how an account like Genesis 16 is assessed.

To explore these and other questions further requires the use of relevant secondary sources, such as commentaries and interpretive aids like Bible dictionaries.

Hagar as Slave and Surrogate

The narrative indicates that Hagar is the slave of Sarai. Possibly, she could be distinguished legally from other slaves, male or female, who are owned by Abram and not Sarai. This is the kind of question that one follows up in looking at the cultural context behind the account as a way to understand the few details about Hagar preserved in it. Let's quickly summarize some of them. First, Sarai proposes to Abram that she give Hagar to him. Second, Hagar's potential pregnancy is described as a way for Sarai to have a child. As Hagar's "mistress" (16:9), Sarai has higher status in the household than Hagar and also considerable authority over her. When Sarai complains to Abram about Hagar, his reply indicates Sarai has power over Hagar's fate (16:6). Third, the angel of the Lord commands Hagar to return specifically to Sarai. These aspects of Hagar's status as distinct from Abram's slaves may not be correct in a legal sense or important to the theme of the narrative, but they make such a status plausible.

Where else might readers go for further exploration of Hagar? A first avenue of approach is other accounts in the HB where Hagar is explicitly named. A concordance or an entry in a Bible dictionary can provide these (Gen. 21:9, 14, 17; 25:2). Perusal of them reveals a second account of conflict in the household, where Hagar and Ishmael are thrust out into the wilderness and God preserves them (Gen. 21:8–21). The reference in 25:2 is part of a list of Ishmael's descendants, including a brief cultural profile of them, and a notice that Ishmael lived 137 years (25:12–18). We shall return to these passages.

As already indicated, a second avenue would include the status and treatment of slaves in ancient Israel and the ANE. Again, one may begin with a commentary on Genesis or an entry in a Bible dictionary (preferably a multi-volume one). Such resources may be adequate in themselves or they may point to more detailed resources. There are texts in the HB dealing with female slaves, but nothing to clarify further Hagar's status as the property of a mistress or as a surrogate to produce an heir for another man's wife. There are, however, are a few cases in surviving Ancient Near Eastern documents that show female slaves as surrogates to produce heirs for another woman.

ABRAM AND SARAI'S CHILDLESSNESS IN THE BOOK OF GENESIS

The subject of Abram and Sarai's progeny is integral to the plot line of the ancestral stories in Genesis 12–50. This portion of Genesis is the larger literary context of the story in Genesis 16.

The narrative that comprises the book of Genesis likely developed over a period of centuries and had several hands as contributors. A general introduction to the HB/OT will rehearse in some detail the theories behind this statement. Our foray through Genesis 16 will intersect only briefly with composition theories for the book. We start with the place of the chapter in the completed book. We described Genesis earlier as comprising two sections: Genesis 1–11 rehearses the origins of the world and people groups in it; Genesis 12–50 tells the story of four generations of the family of Abraham and Sarah as they become a tribal society. A primary theme of Genesis is that God brought the world into being and chose Abraham and Sarah's family as a catalyst for his purposes in it. So the childlessness of Abram and Sarai is no small dilemma!

One of the ways to outline the plot of Genesis is to look for recurring phrases. One phrase that gives an order to the plot is, "these are the generations of." It runs like an organizing thread through the book and connects directly with Ishmael:

2:4	The heavens and the earth
5:1	Adam
6:9	Noah
10:1, 32	Families of Noah's sons
11:10	Shem
11:27	Terah, father of Abram
25:12–13	Ishmael, Abraham's son
25:19	Isaac, Abraham's son

36:1, 9   Esau, Isaac's son
37:2   Jacob

The word translated as "generations" is *toledot*. It is a kinship term and it indicates how important kinship is for defining people groups in Genesis. It seems odd, however, to use the term in 2:4 with reference to the heavens and the earth. Perhaps in this instance the term means something like "account" (NIV) or "story" (NRSV). The term represents connections over time whether the subject is the ongoing history of the heavens and the earth or that of Noah's descendants. One can see, furthermore, in the unfolding plot of Genesis how central is the theme of the developing family line of Terah→Abra(ha)m→Ishmael→ Isaac→Esau→Jacob. Ishmael has a place in it as a son of Abraham and the ancestor of a people group (Ishmaelites). Although the ancestral history of the people of Israel runs through Isaac and Jacob, they are related also to Ishmael through Abraham. So the drama of Genesis 16 plays directly into the larger plot of Genesis to identify people groups in an unfolding national storyline.

With regard to the extended family history in chapters 12 through 50, these introductory words in 12:1–3 represent a primary theme:

> Now the LORD said to Abram, "Go from your country and your kindred and your father's house to the land that I will show you.[2] I will make of you a great nation, and I will bless you, and make your name great, so that you will be a blessing.[3] I will bless those who bless you, and the one who curses you I will curse; and in you all the families of the earth shall be blessed." (NRSV)

These promises require descendants for fulfillment. Many of the stories that follow in Genesis 12–50 explain how they come to pass in spite of obstacles, and they seek to persuade readers of their continuing viability in understanding Israelite identity.

When Abram achieves victory over marauders (Gen. 14), he will remind the Lord that he has neither children nor land (Gen. 15). The account in Genesis 16 follows immediately. After Ishmael is born, the Lord tells Abram that his name will change to Abraham ("father of multitudes") because he will be the ancestor of many nations (17:5). Sarai's name will change name to Sarah ("princess") because she will be the ancestor of kings (17:15–16). A mysterious visitor (remember the angel of the Lord?) reinforces this announcement that Sarah herself will have a son. It seems so strange to her that Sarah laughs (18:1–15). When her son is born, he is called Isaac, the Hebrew term for "laughter" (21:1–7). At this point in the larger narrative, Abraham has two sons, Ishmael and Isaac.

Hagar and Ishmael are again embroiled in conflict in the household of Abraham and they are expelled from it (21:8–21). The account is similar in several respects to that in Genesis 16—so much so that some interpreters think that Genesis 16 and 21:8–21 are two versions of one earlier story. In any case, this second account essentially repeats the claims about Ishmael found in Genesis 16. In 21:8–21, an angel of God assures Hagar that God has "heard" the voice of her boy (Ishmael is not mentioned by name) and that God will make a "great nation" from him. The expulsion of Hagar and Ishmael from Abraham's household, and the announcement that Ishmael is the ancestor of a nation, thus explains how Abraham is the "father of nations," even though the ancestral line for the nation of Israel runs through Isaac and Jacob.

Genesis 22 contains yet another threat to Abraham and Sarah's progeny, this time generated by the strange request of God that Abraham take Isaac, his "only" son, to the land of Moriah and offer him as a sacrifice (Gen. 22). One of the best known dramatic accounts in the Bible, it raises as many questions as it has verses! The threat to Isaac, and thus to the promises made by God to Abraham, are again at center stage in the larger plot of the ancestral stories. Mysteriously, it is God who complicates matters by asking Abraham to sacrifice Isaac, even as God provides an acceptable substitute for the sacrificial offering in light of Abraham's obedient response. The account contains a memorable play on words, that God "sees and provides" (22:8, 14), and repetition from the angel of the Lord that Abraham indeed will have numerous descendants and land for them (22:15–18).

After Sarah dies, Abraham takes another wife. Subsequent children add to the theme that Abraham is the "father of many nations." When he dies, Isaac and Ishmael bury him next to Sarah (25:1–11). The narrator next provides Ishmael's *toledot* (list of "generations") in 25:12–18, followed by the birth account of Isaac's twin sons, Esau and Jacob, in 25:19–26. Thus begins a next cycle of stories dealing with conflict in the Abrahamic family and its growth in the land of Canaan.

BACK AGAIN TO GENESIS 16

We have tried to present some of the characteristics of HB narratives by briefly analyzing Genesis 16 and then putting that chapter into the context of the book of Genesis, its primary literary context. More could be said, but we will conclude this part with some observations for further consideration.

Note the selective specificity of detail in the terseness of the account. Hagar's Egyptian identity distinguishes her from Abram and Sarai. Such a detail might be considered incidental compared to her slave status, if Genesis 16 provided all that survives about her and Ishmael. In 21:21, she chooses an Egyptian wife for Ishmael. Again this choice might incidental. Alternatively, the tribal societies on the fringes of Canaan, known to later readers as Arabs, among other terms, had trading and cultural connections with Egypt. These are the "kin" mentioned in 16:12. In Genesis 37:25–28, Joseph is taken to Egypt by Ishmaelites as a slave. The well of Beer-lahai-roi is another example. The seemingly incidental detail informs later readers how the incident fits the larger storyline. The well appears again in the report that Isaac settled where God "sees" after Abram's death (25:11).

A third example is the chronological notice of Abram's age in 16:16. Why preserve it? In reading the ancestral stories, we fine several reports about the age of a figure like Abram, but we can certainly imagine the story without the detail. Some interpreters conclude that concern for such things is part of the editorial work done by one or more writers during a later stage of transmission, when the stories in Genesis reached final form. Traditionally, these writers concerned with chronological detail are known as the Priestly editors or the Priestly circle. Whether or not this is the best way to explain the chronological details provided in the book of Genesis (and the Pentateuch), such data are not incidental. In the portrayal of Ishmael, they also present a difficulty. He is born when Abram is eighty-six. Isaac is born when Abraham is 100 (21:5). After Isaac is weaned and conflict develops, Hagar and Ishmael are expelled from the household. Ishmael is now a teenager, even though the description of him with Hagar in the wilderness (21:14–20) portrays him as a boy. This is a reminder of the depth dimension or tradition history of many biblical narratives. Their final form comes after a considerable time of preservation and retelling.

We commented earlier on the way in which the angel of the Lord both represented the Lord and spoke as the Lord. These two roles likely reflect a larger conceptual matter in ancient Israel—namely, how does the Lord communicate with people? Can one see the Lord and live? What kind of angel or messenger has authority? In some sense, the supernatural figure in Genesis 16 represents the Lord's direct approach to Hagar, and in another sense, the figure mediates divine presence to her as an authorized representative. Additionally, the term "Lord" renders God's personal name YHWH (sometimes pronounced "Yah-weh") in the HB. In Genesis 21, the supernatural figure is called the "angel of *God*" and speaks for and about God. In Hebrew, as in English, the noun "god" can serve as a personal name or a generic term for deity. Thus, while the two accounts have similar supernatural figures, there is an intriguing difference in terminology. This is another reason that some interpreters have proposed that Genesis 16 and Genesis 21 are variant accounts of an earlier story, with one preferring to use the name YHWH and another preferring the term God. This variation in names is another reminder of the tradition history noted earlier, however one sorts out the complicated question of authorship for these two stories. In their final form they repeat and reinforce the theme of familial conflict and God's overriding of it.

We also commented earlier that the narratives in the HB reflect the remembered history of Israel. That means these stories about a pre-national era are presented with a later national identity in mind. So, the portrayal of Ishmael in Genesis 16 (and Gen. 21) also renders an identity of his descendants for readers. Ishmaelites are characterized, at least in part, as similar to a wild ass—that is, not domesticated or sedentary, and difficult to deal with by neighbors. The stories of Ishmael have an etiological function, therefore, which is to explain the origins of Ishmaelites and related tribal peoples. Genesis has several of these accounts, connecting the origins of Israelite neighbors to Terah and Abraham, including the Moabites and Ammonites (Gen. 19:30–38), the Midianites (25:1–4), and the Edomites (36:1–43).

GENESIS 38

We encounter another story about a family dilemma in Genesis 38. Here is an outline of its contents:

    I. Judah and his family   38:1–5
      A. Judah marries a daughter of Shua   38:1–2
      B. Er, first-born son   38:3
      C. Onan, second-born son   38:4
      D. Shelah, third-born son   38:5
   II. Er marries Tamar   38:6
  III. Problem of childlessness and initial actions   38:7–10
      A. Wicked Er dies childless   38:7
      B. Onan is surrogate for widow Tamar   38:8
      C. Onan dies, no heir   38:9–10
      D. Shelah is promised as surrogate but withheld   38:11a
      E. Tamar lives as widow; no heir for Er and Judah   38:11b
 IV. The Problem of childlessness in Judah's line
     remains   38:12–23
      A. Judah widowed and travels to Timnah 38:12
      B. Tamar meets Judah as veiled, unknown
         woman   38:13–15
      C. Judah gives items as pledge to pay for sex   38:16–18a
      D. Tamar conceives and leaves with pledged
         items   38:18b–19
      E. Judah finds neither prostitute nor pledged
         items   38:20–23
    V. The Problem of a pregnant, widowed
     daughter-in-law   38:24–26
      A. Judah pronounces judgment on pregnant
         Tamar   38:24
      B. She produces pledged items to reveal the father   38:25
      C. Tamar is more righteous than Judah   38:26
  VI. The birth of Perez and Zerah to Tamar (and
     Judah)   38:27–30

Initial Observations about Genesis 38

This is a suspenseful, entertaining narrative with drama, dilemma, death, sex, a family trial, and the birth of twins. Quite a presentation in thirty verses of text! In defining the dilemma, we will pick up the plot and character portrayal. Judah marries and has three sons. The oldest, Er, marries Tamar. A "wicked" man, Er dies childless. This is the dilemma: Er has no children. Here's the proposed solution: Judah instructs his second son Onan to "perform the duties of a brother-in-law" and thus to "raise up offspring" (i.e., an heir) for Er. As with the matter of Hagar and surrogacy, the narrative presupposes older customs regarding marriage, children, and inheritance. Onan self-consciously fails, is judged by God, and dies. Judah, fearful for the continuation of his family, withholds his last son from the role of raising an offspring for Er. Tamar is literally set aside.

Now a widower, Judah takes a business trip. The dilemma remains. Tamar plays the role of a veiled prostitute along the roadway and Judah partakes of her services, giving her personal items in pledge until he can return from town to provide payment. She absconds with the items.

Months later, when Judah learns that Tamar is pregnant, he orders that she be brought out in public and burned for harlotry. She then produces Judah's pledged items and declares that he is the father in question. Judah responds that Tamar is more "righteous" than he because he did not give her to his surviving son Shelah. The account concludes with the birth of twin sons and a resolution to the family's dilemma of no heir(s).

Although important to the story, Judah's three sons are not developed characters. None of them speaks. There are other, unnamed speakers in the account. Judah's voice is the dominant one in the narrative, but Tamar's actions provide the suspense and drive the account to its conclusion. The narrator is authoritative in knowing God's assessment of Er and Onan.

There are several wordplays on names in the text (e.g., 38:7, 28–30).

The Surrogacy of Brothers

Judah's words and (in-)actions show him to be a patriarchal figure who recognizes his responsibility to raise offspring for his deceased, childless son (38:8–11, 26). In this instance, there are other biblical texts that provide data on what we called the dilemma of the story. The primary text is Deuteronomy 25:5–10, where in the case of a deceased man with no son, his brother is to take the surviving widow in marriage for the purpose of providing an heir for the deceased. The passage is formulated as a case law for the nation of Israel. Interpreters have given the marital arrangement the name "Levirite marriage," based on the Latin word for "brother-in-law." As we shall see, the book of Ruth presents a similar dilemma in narrative form, where a deceased Israelite's widow is married to another male member of his family (not a brother-in-law) in order to provide an heir.

At this point, we note a couple of matters related to narrative interpretation. The first is that historical narratives in the HB typically reflect the customs and laws of Israelite identity. First, Genesis 38 presupposes a family ethos, and the case law in Deuteronomy 25:5–10 is instruction in a covenant code for the nation of Israel. In the story of Ruth, there is no surviving case law that matches the circumstances of the account, but the marriage of Ruth and Boaz coheres with the cultural values of Deuteronomy 25:5–10. Second, both case law and narrative reflect tension in the possible actions of family members. In Genesis 38, we encounter a father and son who do not follow through on customary obligation. In Deuteronomy 25, the case law explicitly recognizes that a brother-in-law may not wish to engage in Levirite marriage.

Note that the case law has a shaming mechanism carried out by the widow to deal with a recalcitrant brother-in-law. In Genesis 38, Tamar's actions, including the subterfuge of prostitution, bring Judah to confess that she is more righteous than he. His affirmation is not an endorsement of prostitution but, rather, praise for her commitment to her dead husband's line, which exceeded his own commitment. She risked death in order to perpetuate the family line, while he avoided that same risk by keeping Tamar from Shelah.

There is much for modern readers to ponder regarding human identity and purpose in the ancient marriage customs depicted in Genesis 16 and 38. These matters are mediated through action and speech, which "explain" ancestral history, even as the accounts seek to persuade readers that they are part of a larger purpose in God's formation of a people.

JUDAH AND TAMAR IN THE BOOK OF GENESIS

Tamar is introduced in Genesis 38 and nothing is preserved about her origins. Judah is the son of Jacob, the son of Isaac. His identity in the book, therefore, furthers the plot and theme of Abraham's descendants as a nation-to-be. We will return to Tamar momentarily. Surprisingly, Genesis 38 interrupts a presentation of stories about Joseph, another son of Jacob. This may seem artless as a presentation. Possibly, Genesis 38 is a later insertion in the Joseph cycle (Gen. 37, 39–50). Nevertheless, we might see the account in a somewhat different contextual light, if we think of Genesis 37–50 as a cycle of stories about Joseph and his brothers—the next generation after Jacob, which also faced threats to its existence. In any case, as the chapters now stand, the stories of Joseph and Judah show how the line of Abraham survives threats to his continuance and even flourishes.

Judah is the fourth son of Jacob and Leah (Gen. 29:35) and the ancestor of one of the twelve tribes of Israel. In Jacob's blessing of Judah's descendants, the Judahites will receive praise from their brothers and royal rule will emerge from them (Gen. 49:8–12). This picks up on the promise made to Sarai that kings would come forth from her (Gen. 17:16). These two references hint at what later readers will immediately recognize: King David was from the tribe of Judah. As we shall see, Tamar's son Perez is David's ancestor (1 Chron. 2:1–17; the book of Ruth). This puts the dilemma of Genesis 38 in bold relief! Its plot intersects not only with that of the larger book of Genesis but also with the larger storyline of Israel's history.

3

Plot and Theme in the Book of Ruth

THE BOOK OF RUTH IS a short story in four chapters. As such, it is longer than the narrative accounts in Genesis 16 or 38, but shorter than the cycle of stories regarding Abraham and Sarai or those about Joseph and his brothers. Please read the book in at least two different translations. How might you initially describe the plot and theme(s) of the book?

Here is an outline of the book.

1:1–5	Famine, migration, and death in the family of Elimelech
1:6–18	Naomi and Ruth return from Moab to Judah
1:19–22	Naomi and Ruth settle in Bethlehem at barley harvest
2:1–7	Ruth gleans in the field of Boaz, a kinsman of her deceased husband
2:8–16	Boaz assists and protects Ruth in the public realm
2:17–23	Naomi urges Ruth to continue gleaning in Boaz's field
3:1–5	Naomi urges Ruth to have an evening meeting with Boaz

3:6–13	Ruth startles Boaz and urges him to consider marrying her
3:14–18	Naomi and Ruth wait for Boaz to deal with family matters
4:1–12	Boaz acquires Elimelech's property and marries Ruth
4:13–17	Obed is born to Boaz and Ruth
4:18–22	The genealogy of Perez leads to David

It is no simple task to provide an outline of a narrative of this size. A helpful one could take several forms. In this one, Ruth is a bit different from those for the shorter accounts in Genesis 16 and 38. Most of the entries could easily be supplemented with subpoints. Why construct an outline at all? As noted previously, it is a way for an interpreter to work through a narrative and to begin describing plot and theme. An outline can be a work in progress, like the task of interpreting the narrative itself.

We noted earlier the prominence of speaking in biblical narratives. The book of Ruth is no exception. Speech makes up the majority of it. The dialogue between characters can be outlined, but that task is difficult to do while also outlining the sequence of events. It can make an outline too large or cumbersome. In this outline, the emphasis is on a sequence of events to keep the storyline in view.

Bible translations present books not only in chapter and verse but also in paragraphs. Chapters and verses are decisions made by past editors on behalf of readers, reaching back centuries into the past. Paragraphs in a modern translation can be influenced by past versions, but they are finally the decision of a modern editorial committee. Chapters and paragraphs influence the way we assimilate and understand biblical narratives, just they do in reading the *Iliad* or a modern novel. What we think of as an event (or related events) or a scene is often presented to us as a chapter or a paragraph in biblical narratives. This was the case in Genesis 16 and 38. In the outline here, several of its headings correspond to paragraph demarcations in a modern translation (NRSV) or what appears to be a scene (a discrete event or a dialogue between characters) in the larger story.

PLOT AND DILEMMA: SOME INITIAL THOUGHTS

Attention to dilemma or conflict in a narrative helps put its plot in relief. Ruth's initial paragraph of five verses summarizes ten or more years of a nuclear family's history and its difficulties. There was famine in Judah, so Elimelech and Naomi and their two sons migrate to Moab. While there, Elimelech dies. The sons marry Moabite women and then they die. Of the original four, Naomi alone remains, along with her daughters-in-law. As the plot develops, we learn that the childlessness of Mahlon and Ruth—and thus also the lack of an heir for Elimelech and Naomi—is a dilemma resolved with the birth of Obed to Ruth and Boaz. And what a story it will be to get to Obed's birth!

Given the terseness of the introductory paragraph, there are a host of unanswered questions, only some of which are addressed later in the narrative. Let's look at a few questions as ways to explore plot. They will lead to related matters of theme and point of view.

WHY GO TO MOAB BECAUSE OF A FAMINE IN JUDAH?

The narrator pairs the famine with the migration, as if to say that one led to the other. Geography and ethnicity play important roles in the story, however one answers the question. Ruth's

Moabite heritage is repeatedly mentioned, as is Bethlehem of Judah, the home of Elimelech's family. Why leave Bethlehem and go to Moab? Later details in the story may offer a reason. Boaz purchases a field that belonged to Elimelech, his dead kinsman (4:1–10). We are told that Naomi has the field for sale and that the purchase is an act of redemption. We are not told that the property had been a support to Naomi (or Ruth) after her return from Moab, nor are we told explicitly that Boaz paid her for the property. The legal matters regarding family and property in the book of Ruth are quite complicated, but for the moment the redemption of the property by Boaz may be best described in modern terms as the payment of a lien (a debt), so that full use of the property could be restored to Elimelech's heirs.

A connection between famine and Elimelech's migration to Moab may be as follows: The famine that struck Bethlehem meant that Elimelech could not produce enough food and/or income from his familial property. He borrowed against the value of it in order to provide for his family, thus placing the future productive use of his land (but not its ownership) in the hands of a creditor until he could pay off the loan. When he was unable to make ends meet or to pay off his loan, he migrated with his wife and sons to Moab. It must be stressed that this "explanation" is hypothetical and that it may be incorrect. Exploring the question is an exercise in following the plot and asking about the connection of details. It involves questions arising from the text itself and pushes us as readers to explore matters in the world behind the text, where possible. Readers in ancient Israel—the intended audience of the narrator—may simply have nodded their heads, recognizing a common dilemma where subsistence farming and herding runs up against destabilizing forces. Elimelech had accumulated debts in hard times and departed for a fresh start, and Naomi was in a tight spot upon her return after his death. It is also possible that we as later readers are unable to untangle the connection between certain details in a tersely told tale, whatever earlier audiences surmised about it. Furthermore, the narrator presents a story from the past and either may not know a connection between some of the inherited details or may not present them accurately. It is clear, for example, that the story is told about an earlier time (1:1, 4:7).

What about Ruth's Moabite heritage? Would the story be essentially the same if the family had gone instead to Gilead or Hebron or Tyre? Ruth plays several roles in the account (e.g., breadwinner, widow, wife, mother), but her Moabite identity is repeatedly noted in it. It marks her otherness in Bethlehem. She is a foreigner, even if she is the widow of Mahlon. Nevertheless, her Moabite identity does not impede her place in the family of Elimelech in Bethlehem. But could (or should) it impede her place in the family? Have we perhaps identified a theme in the story—that being a foreigner is not a detriment to a place in the life of Judah? The Lord can use a Moabite woman for great things in Israel. Her contribution to the family of Perez, a prominent clan in Judah (4:18–22), is crucial, even as she provides an heir for her dead husband and a redeemer for her mother-in-law.

Here is where we ask a question that is "behind the text," but motivated by a close reading of the book itself. Given what we can learn about Moab and the relationship between Moabites and Israelites, is there something in that history that might assist us further in engaging this story? There are several connections between Moab, Israel, and Judah in the HB, and these are readily summarized in a Bible dictionary. The book of Deuteronomy conveniently assists us with some relevant data for our question. It draws on traditions in the book of Genesis that the Moabites are related to Israel through the family of Terah and Abraham (Gen. 19; Deut. 2:1–25). More specifically, they are descendants of Lot, Abraham's nephew. There is, however, bad blood between Moab and Israel. No Moabite is to be admitted to the assembly of the Lord in Israel (Deut. 23:3–6). How does the story of Ruth the Moabite fit with this prohibition? And here is a separate, but related question: Is it possible that the book was written as a corrective to the prohibition? Think of elements in the storyline: Yes, Ruth was Moabite, but she freely and unreservedly committed herself to the family and the religion of Elimelech (Ruth 1:16–17). Boaz commended her and expressed hope that Ruth would receive a reward from the Lord, under whose wings she had come to dwell (2:11–12). And she is the great grandmother of King David (4:17). Is this the kind of Moabite who should be excluded from the cultic life of Israel?

Some commentators on the book of Ruth have concluded that it is intended to counter forms of religious exclusivism in Israel by presenting an account of what a Moabite woman contributes to Israel's life at an early point in tribal existence. We'll explore this further in chapter 8, when looking at some texts in Ezra and Nehemiah. During the period of Persian rule (5th–4th centuries BCE), leaders of the struggling Jewish community in Jerusalem instituted divorces between Jewish men and their non-Jewish wives in an attempt to purify and to preserve the nation. Moabites and the exclusive passage from Deuteronomy are cited explicitly (Neh. 13:1–3, 23–31; cf. Ezra 10:1–44). These observations are part of a world-behind-the-text exploration.[1] At the moment, let's say that we have identified a plausible theme for the story and a purpose for the book.

In asking about the plot, we've also been exploring the author's point of view—how the account is framed. And we have suggested a theme for the story: foreigners can be valuable contributors to Israel's identity. This suggested theme may be flawed, at least to the extent that it was not the author's intention to counter exclusive marriage customs in the Persian period. Ruth's Moabite heritage is not an incidental detail in the account, however we evaluate the migration to Moab and her inclusion in the tribe of Judah. Questions about Moab and marriage led us to put the book of Ruth in a larger conversation with the books of Deuteronomy, Ezra, and Nehemiah, even if Ruth did not originate as a counter to forms of religious exclusivism. Remember the analogy of siblings from the introduction? Israel placed each of these books in its family collection. Reading one in conversation with the other is what family members do.

ELIMELECH'S FAMILY IDENTITY?

We might think of this question as a part of character analysis, a form of approach that we will undertake in the next chapter. In Elimelech's case, the topic serves as an early clue to the plot of the book. His death comes in 1:3, so for his identity we have little to go on by way of actions and nothing by way of speaking. His recorded two acts—the moving of the family to Moab and his death—do set important things in motion and his family identity is foundational to the story as it unfolds. The narrator tells us that Elimelech was from Bethlehem in Judah and that he was an Ephrathite. These turn out to be important markers, and we shall return to them momentarily. He also lived during the days of the Judges—that is, before the rise of monarchy in Israel, a later period obviously known to the narrator and the intended audience, who are looking back at remembered history.

The narrative is silent about Naomi's reception upon her return to Bethlehem. Why were there no family members to meet her and to assist her? Where did she and Ruth live? Ruth's endeavor to gather grain for food results in her gleaning stalks of barley in a field belonging to man named Boaz (2:1–3). He is a member of Elimelech's extended family or clan. Surprisingly the terms used to describe Boaz here and elsewhere in the book do not specify further his relationship to Elimelech. Ruth just "happened" to appear on his property, as the narrator puts it. One could infer that Naomi and Ruth schemed to meet Elimelech's kinsman, but the narrator's mysterious comment more naturally implies that Ruth did not end up there by human design, but by the working of God's will. In conversation, Boaz indicates that he knows what Ruth has done so far for Naomi and he offers a blessing upon Ruth, but says nothing about his kinship with Elimelech.

Naomi informs Ruth that Boaz is Elimelech's relative and one who can serve as a "kinsman-redeemer" (2:20; Heb. *go'el*). Again, the vague description does not assist us as readers in determining how Boaz is Elimelech's kin, only that he is eligible to play an important role in family affairs. Kinsman-redeemer is a term used several other times in the book and refers to a function in which a male family member vindicates, rescues, or ransoms another family member. We will discuss this term further in chapter 6. After the dramatic encounter at the threshing floor, where Ruth implores Boaz to play the role of kinsman-redeemer, we learn that there is an unnamed relative of Elimelech, closer to Elimelech in family structure than Boaz. This unnamed relative gives up his right as redeemer to Boaz (4:1–6). Ruth marries Boaz, who is related somehow to her deceased husband Mahlon and her deceased father-in-law. The family of Elimelech and Mahlon will continue through the child born to Ruth and Boaz.

We may contrast the opaqueness of Boaz's lineage connection to Elimelech with the blessing offered on his marriage to Ruth. It comes from assembled witnesses:

> May the LORD make the woman who is coming into your house
> like Rachel and Leah, who together built up the house of Israel.
> May you produce children in Ephrathah and bestow a name in

Bethlehem;[12] and, through the children that the LORD will give you by this young woman, may your house be like the house of Perez, whom Tamar bore to Judah. (4:11–12; NRSV)

This blessing and the genealogy at the book's conclusion indicate that Elimelech's family is the house of Perez. That is possibly the name of the clan mentioned in 2:3. In any case, Boaz is from that same clan. The child born to him and Ruth, while continuing the line of Mahlon, is also reckoned as Boaz's son and part of the descent from Judah to David through Perez. As the plot develops, therefore, the family identity of Elimelech is revealed. We should note also the reference to Rachel, Leah, and Tamar in the wedding blessing. The short story of Ruth is linked with earlier tribal history, portions of which are preserved in the ancestral accounts of Genesis. More particularly, the book of Ruth and Genesis 38 share a dramatic motif: two women who defy custom and who prod male family members into providing what is necessary in their culture for the continuation of the family line. Tamar, likely a Canaanite, plays the part of a prostitute. The other, a Moabite, uncovers a male family member with the request for marriage and the redemption of family assets.

We return to the book's initial paragraph and the description of Elimelech as an Ephrathite from Bethlehem. In contrast with the opaqueness in the narrative regarding how he and Boaz are related, this early detail stands out. Ephrathah is both a clan name and a geographic name in the HB. The two references in Ruth (1:2, 4:11) are most naturally taken as a geographic name related to the town of Bethlehem. Only two other people in the HB are identified as Ephrathites from Bethlehem. They are Jesse and his son David (1 Sam. 17:12). This common identification could be a coincidence, but given the other connections to David in the book of Ruth, Elimelech's initial family description in 1:1–2 is likely an allusion to his family's wider significance. We should note another connection with Ephrathah and Bethlehem and royal rule. Micah 5:2 preserves a prophecy that Bethlehem of Ephrathah, a small clan of Judah, shall produce a ruler for Israel whose origin is from ancient days. This is not a prophecy about the coming rule of David but, rather, about someone from his line who would rise to rule Israel. The book of Micah is centuries later than the period of David's life, and its prophecy is one of several associated with future rulers from David's line in different prophetic books (e.g., Isa. 9:1–7; Amos 9:11–12; Hosea 3:5).

The narrative of Ruth, therefore, intersects with the larger remembered history of Israel, reaching back to ancestral lore embedded in the book of Genesis and pointing forward narratively to the rule of David over the tribes of Israel. It connects specifically with the account of Tamar and the birth of Perez, sharing the common motif of the woman who defies custom to further the family line. It also represents a theme common to both—namely, that God would use the family line of Judah to produce a ruler to bless the people of Israel.

HOW DOES RUTH'S MARRIAGE TO BOAZ ALLEVIATE A DILEMMA?

Ruth's marriage to Boaz is both central to the plot of the book and perhaps the most difficult matter in it conceptually for modern readers to grasp. One wonders how much of the difficulty resides in a cultural distance from ancient social institutions and the extent to which the intended audience understood connections that are not otherwise explained. In any case, a dilemma set up in the opening paragraph comes to a legal resolution with their marriage and the birth of Obed. The son fulfills the task indicated for marrying Ruth: he raises up the name of the deceased upon his inheritance (4:5,

10). Naomi, furthermore, who had complained bitterly about God's treatment of her as an "empty" widow (1:20–21), now has a kinsman-redeemer in her grandson (4:14–15). These roles for Obed relate directly to the nuclear family of Elimelech, introduced in the opening paragraph as facing biological extinction. Still, there are complicating matters arising from the narrative itself. Whose name is now established on his inheritance and represented in Obed? Is it Elimelech and/or Mahlon (Ruth's first husband)? The redemption of the property belonging to Elimelech is related to the marriage between Boaz and Ruth, but how are the property and marriage related? Obed is also reckoned as Boaz's son. How does that work legally and in extended family dynamics? Again, these are complicated matters raised by a close reading of the text, but which require explorations elsewhere if they are to be answered (at all).

In terms of plot development, the question of marriage surfaces dramatically in the nocturnal encounter between Ruth and Boaz at the threshing floor (3:7–9). Indeed, it was hinted at in the previous scene, where Naomi tells Ruth that she is concerned that her daughter-in-law can find "rest" (3:1; cf. 1:9) and security, and thus she instructs Ruth to go to the threshing floor and uncover Boaz's feet. As Naomi puts it, "He will tell you what to do" (3:4). In a role-reversal response, after uncovering his feet, Ruth tells Boaz what to do. Specifically, she asks that he spread the hem of his garment over her because he can fulfill the role of kinsman-redeemer (3:9). The reference to "spreading the hem of a garment" is an idiomatic expression for holding the cover of a marital bed for a wife (Deut. 22:17; Ezek. 16:8). In essence, Ruth asks that he marry her and fulfill the role of kinsman-redeemer for Elimelech's line. Boaz understands her request in this context of family loyalty, commends her for it, and goes to the gate of Bethlehem to meet with an unnamed kinsman (Mr. So-and-so), who is more closely related to Elimelech than he.

The marriage blessing offered to Boaz and Ruth by towns-people (4:11–12, quoted earlier) puts their union in the context of tribal and national history. However we sort out the legal matters regarding property and marriage customs, the plot moves toward this affirmation: in marriage they can "build the house" of Israel as did Rachel and Leah, the wives of Jacob and the mothers of the eponymous tribal ancestors. As with Judah and Tamar, the surprising union of Boaz and Ruth furthers the national storyline. Boaz is the great-grandfather of King David, according to the genealogy at the book's conclusion, which lists the *toledot* ("generations") of Perez like the repeated lists in the book of Genesis. Here is the narrator's point of view at work, explaining the significance of Israel's remembered history.

As indicated earlier, the parallels between the two stories of Ruth and Tamar constitute a literary motif, an entertaining use of a common subject. Let's call it the "motif of the surprising surrogate." Here are basic elements to it in tabular form.

I.   The problem of no family heir (Judah/Er, Elimelech/Mahlon)
II. Difficulty in customary means of redressing the problem (Onan, Mr. So-and-so)
III. The surprising contributions of (foreign) women in the family to alleviate the problem
IV. The birth of a significant figure through surrogacy (Perez, Obed)

Surrogacy simply means "substitute." In Genesis 38, the brother of the deceased is assigned the customary responsibility of taking the surviving sister-in-law in marriage to provide an heir. This is paralleled in the case law of Deuteronomy (25:5–10), but it is assumed in the surprising narrative that other family members could play a role in resolving the family dilemma. It is clear also that such an arrangement could have a downside in family life, inheritance rights, and the like for those involved. This is explicit in Onan's actions and those of Mr. So-and-so (not a brother-in-law), who initially wanted to acquire the Elimelech's property to which he was entitled, yet decided against the purchase once he saw that marriage to Ruth was linked to it. Perhaps he reckoned that the property would revert to a son born of their union, who would represent Elimelech's line, even though he had paid to redeem it. The case law in Deuteronomy is also telling on this point. A surviving brother may not wish to complicate his life and that of his nuclear family; thus, a shaming mechanism is offered as a possible response of the widow. The marriage of Boaz and Ruth could solve a problem for Elimelech's family, yet lead to others for Boaz. The narrative is silent on this point and we shall return to it in the analysis of their characters in the next chapter. We should note here the similarities with the story of Hagar in Genesis 16. She, too, was a surrogate and her pregnancy with Ishmael was the source of family friction.

The efforts of Tamar and Ruth are both entertaining and dramatic. In both cases, they run against aspects of law and custom. Tamar's "prostitution" led to family prosecution. Boaz is keen for Ruth's nocturnal visit not to be known (Ruth 3:14), as charges of prostitution or deceit could be lodged against her. As noted earlier, Tamar is likely a Canaanite woman, although this is not stated explicitly in Genesis 38. Ruth's Moabite heritage is central to her character. Both women, nevertheless, show the highest commitment to their husband's family.

CONCLUDING REFLECTIONS ON PLOT, THEME, AND POINT OF VIEW IN RUTH

We have proposed two themes of significance in discussing the plot. One is the contribution of a foreigner (a Moabite woman) to the family history of Judah. The other is the theme of God at work in Judah's tribal history to prepare for the birth of King

David. Perhaps there are others? These two grow out of the narrative itself, and they intersect with other traditions in the HB. There is much explanation and persuasion at work in the book. We'll have occasion to revisit elements from this discussion, as we look at character development in the next chapter.

On several occasions we've had opportunity to note the cultural distance between our location as modern readers and the narrator's intended audience in ancient Israel. This is not to denigrate the past but, rather, to underscore the effort needed from our side to engage the story with openness. Let's look one more time at a matter of family identity represented in the book's narrative. The redemption sought by Ruth was not simply to provide for Naomi in her old age or for herself. It concerned also loyalty to her dead husband and perhaps to Elimelech as well. Even in death, his/their place in the family line mattered. Naomi offers a blessing on Boaz and thanks God for kindness shown to the living and the dead (2:20). The "dead" would include her husband and two sons. The living included Ruth and herself. In providing food for her and Ruth, the living-and-dead family had not been forsaken. Boaz married Ruth in order to maintain or establish the name of the dead on his inheritance (4:5, 10). In some corporate sense, Mahlon and Elimelech would continue as long as their "name" (identity) was maintained and their inheritance defined. Familial and personal identities are thus thickly intertwined in the narrative. Modern perceptions of individual identity and personal autonomy make it more difficult to grasp the assumptions that drive the plot and the commitments that the characters make (more on this in the next chapter). There is also the patriarchalism of family structure in the ancient culture that can inhibit our appreciation of the dynamics at work in the story. From a modern perspective we can say that Ruth was every bit the kinswoman-redeemer, even if the ancient culture (and thus the narrative) does not grant her this title!

4

Characters in
the Book of Ruth

RECALL THE SUGGESTED ANALOGY BETWEEN a cut diamond and a text. In the last chapter, we looked at the book of Ruth and related narratives through some "facets" to consider matters of plot, theme, and point of view. We now move to some other facets to consider matters of character analysis.

The book of Ruth has a considerable list of characters for a biblical narrative of its size. Some of the minor or less developed characters may not register with readers on an initial reading, but they contribute in various ways to the narrator's "jewel." Here are the characters in list form, something like the cast list for a play or movie:

Elimelech
Naomi
Mahlon
Chilion
Orpah
God
Ruth
Women in Bethlehem
Boaz
Reapers

Foreman
Male reapers
10 elders
Mr. So-and-so (Elimelech's closer kin)
Assembled people
Obed

These are all characters who appear in the narrative. There are others mentioned in the genealogy (Ruth 4:18–22). Does the narrative have one major character? This is an interesting question! It has three major characters, if "major" is measured by the size of their roles. These would be Naomi, Ruth, and Boaz. If there is *a* lead character, one could make a good case for Ruth. The fact that the book bears her name would support such a conclusion. One can make a good case also for Naomi, a developed figure who represents the living and dead members of the family in question. Boaz, too, is central to the plot, with a well-differentiated role and a place in the concluding genealogy. Perhaps it is better to think of multiple major characters in the story, those whose speaking and acting roles are more developed, along with minor characters, those whose roles are less developed, without thinking too specifically of rank. After all, we are not dealing with a professional production where pay scale and marquee lists are paramount matters. As noted in a previous discussion, we might describe the major characters as round and the minor characters as flat, but this way of evaluating is best done as part of a continuum (and in relation to other characters) rather than as a linear ranking. Elimelech and his sons, for example, have nothing to say and all die in the introduction. As flat characters they are nevertheless influential to the plot and the defining of a family with a national identity. And then there is the question of divine activity. God acts explicitly and implicitly in the story. How do we assess that role?

CHARACTERIZATION AND POINT OF VIEW

Let's examine some of the minor characters in the narrative as an initial way to explore a literary portrait and point of view in characterization. By point of view we don't mean in the first instance the narrator's opinion but, rather, the manner in which a character is rendered and then placed or framed in the larger story.

On two different occasions, the women of Bethlehem speak (1:19, 4:14). They are flat characters, voices from a village setting to add texture to the story. There are parallels to such characters in the story of Judah and Tamar in Genesis 38. When Judah asks about a prostitute near the town of Timnah, the inhabitants simply reply that no such person has been seen recently (38:20–21). Later, an unnamed source reports to Judah that Tamar has played the harlot and is pregnant (38:24). These voices in Genesis 38 have the deft role of confirming the narrative tension that the "prostitution" under consideration is not associated with Timnah but, instead, emerged from within Judah's larger household. Readers might wonder which person(s) in Judah's circle gossiped about Tamar, but the narrator provides no additional details. As flat characters, essentially disembodied voices, they further the suspense of the narrative through what they say and they confirm certain things about a major character.

The women of Bethlehem function similarly and their collective voice assists in interpreting major characters. They first speak on the occasion of Naomi and Ruth's entrance to Bethlehem. The narrator frames the scene with the report that the whole town is stirred up by the arrival of the two women from Moab. The women of Bethlehem, possibly representing the voice of the inhabitants, ask: "Is this Naomi?" Naomi replies to them that she should no longer be called *Naomi* (based on the Hebrew word for "pleasant"), but *Mara* (based on the Hebrew word for "bitter"). Her explanation is that God has dealt harshly with her. Previously she left Bethlehem full, but now returns empty (1:20–21; cf. 1:13).[1] The brief question of the Bethlehem women, therefore, provides the occasion for a major character to identify herself to them and to underscore the dilemma of the plot. Note, furthermore, that it is in speaking that Naomi is rendered. It is the primary way she is presented in the narrative, just as it will be for Ruth and Boaz. She employs a wordplay in self-definition and charges God with bringing disaster upon her. A modern novel has several ways to say directly to readers that such and such a character is depressed and angry. More often than not, readers are led to such personal evaluations of biblical characters through described actions and reported speech. So it is with Naomi. The narrator does not say that Naomi was angry or sad of heart, but renders her that way through speech.

The women of Bethlehem speak to Naomi a second time (4:14–15):

> Blessed be the LORD, who has not left you this day without next-of-kin; and may his name be renowned in Israel! He shall be to you a restorer of life and a nourisher of your old age; for your daughter-in-law who loves you, who is more to you than seven sons, has borne him. (NRSV)

There are several ways in which this quote reframes Naomi's earlier bitter response to them. Whereas Naomi lamented God's bitter treatment of her, the women bless the Lord who has provided for Naomi in her old age. Whereas Naomi claimed to return to Bethlehem empty—even though Ruth was with her—the women celebrate what her daughter-in-law has now accomplished for her. Whereas, Naomi advocated a name change because of her bitterness, the women express hope that the name of her redeemer will be renown in Israel. This is the rendering of Naomi through blessing by minor characters. The women do not drive the plot, but they interpret it through their characterization of other figures in the narrative. Their words take into account the beneficent actions of Ruth and Boaz, even when Naomi receives the majority of attention in the narrative's final scene.

Are there other things that might be said about the women of Bethlehem and their characterization? Possibly so, and here is one that is speculative. The book of Ruth has more about female characters and gender roles than many of the stories in the HB. Is there any significance to the role of women speaking as a group? It is rather uncommon for a speaking group to be so designated in the HB. Consider, for example, the minor characters mentioned above in Genesis 38. The gender of the speakers from Timnah or from the household of Judah is neither indicated nor does it seem called for in the terse narrative. Perhaps the corporate female voice in Ruth is just a coincidence or something embedded the story, re-presented by the narrator, and then passed along in written form. Perhaps their voice represents the segment of village culture available to Naomi in her social context; as a single female, her social intercourse may have been largely limited to other women. We might, however, look at the characterization of speaking women in light of the question, who tells a story like that in the book of Ruth, a story with developed female characters, a story where a mother-in-law shares center stage? One possible answer is that village and clan matriarchs told stories like these and that their point of view is reflected not only the characterization of Naomi and Ruth but also in the corporate female voice of Bethlehem.

As we noted earlier, Elimelech, Chilion, and Mahlon are Ephrathites from Bethlehem, ancestors of King David. What else can be said about their characterization? Again, we might look to Genesis 38 for comparison. In that narrative, male family also die in the beginning of the account. The narrator explicitly describes Er as wicked and that God judged him with death (38:7). Indeed, his name is a play on the Hebrew word for evil. According to the narrator, the actions of his brother Onan were also displeasing to the Lord and he too was judged with death (38:10). The deaths of these flat characters are foundational to the story of Tamar and Judah and the surprising way that the line of Judah continues. In the cases of Elimelech and his sons, no direct evaluation is presented—that is, the narrator does provide God's disposition toward them or describe them as wicked. What might we say, then, about the characterization of them?

The terseness of their description and the lack of explicit evaluation are characteristic of narratives in the HB. We might, therefore, reformulate the question and ask whether there are any clues in the narrative to evaluate their characters and to allow the implied audience to draw some conclusions about them? Their clan identity as Judahites is positive. Perhaps we simply acknowledge their death as tragic and difficult for the surviving family members, while recognizing that the plotline presents a surprising way for this significant family to continue. Several aspects of the narrative frame the report of the three deaths and possibly characterize the three men:

1. These events happened in the days of the judges.
2. Famine struck Bethlehem.
3. The family moved to Moab.
4. Mahlon and Chilion married Moabite women and had no children.

The implied audience might see negative connotations in one or more of these things and infer that they tainted Elimelech and his sons. The book of Judges presents the life of tribal Israel as a pattern of failure, divine judgment, repentance, and restoration. Indeed, to read the book is to encounter cycles of this pattern. Famine occurs repeatedly in the narratives of the HB and, at times, is presented as judgment from God (e.g., 2 Sam. 24:10–14). It can drive people to leave their surroundings, with the result that life among foreigners becomes threatening. This was the case in the ancestral stories for Abram (Gen. 12:10–20), Isaac (Gen. 26:1–11), and most significantly in the storyline of the HB, the descendants of Jacob, who went to Egypt because of a famine and became slaves for generations. Relations between Israel and Moab had periodic downsides, and the religion of Moab was a corrupting influence on Solomon, who had a Moabite wife (1 Kings 11:1–8). The lack of offspring can be understood as divine judgment or limitation. Recall, for example, Sarai's comment that the Lord had prevented her from conceiving (Gen. 16:2).

None of these things necessarily characterizes Elimelech and his sons as failures or wicked, although some interpreters of the book have so concluded. The implied audience may not have assumed that the cyclical pattern presented in Judges applied to Elimelech's family in the sense of failure and needed repentance. A famine in Judah is not necessarily a judgment on inhabitants. And there is no compelling reason to see the sojourn in Moab as debilitating or corrupting the family. Ruth's Moabite heritage is not presented as an impediment to life in the clan of Perez and the tribe of Judah. The pattern of famine, threat, and deliverance from the ancestral stories might characterize Elimelech and his sons without implying personal failure or wickedness on their part. Just like Judah of old, they moved elsewhere to get food. The Lord saw to the continuation of their family, even when the men died. Having said all this, the intended audience (and the subtle narrator) may well have seen Elimelech's move as faithless, the marriage of his sons to Moabites as wrong, and the death of all three as judgment upon them.

A good reading strategy looks carefully for clues in characterization and how figures are framed. That is the point to stress, however one assesses Elimelech and his sons.

CHARACTERS IN CONTRAST

The book of Ruth presents three pairs of characters who play off one another:

> Ruth and Orpah
> Ruth and Naomi
> Boaz and Mr. So-and-so

Interaction between characters is basic to narratives. Events often connect through relationships between characters. There is, furthermore, the aspect of role in relationships. Take, for example, the intrepid detective Sherlock Holmes in the novels by Sir Arthur Conan Doyle, whose companion, Dr. Watson, is of a different temperament and possesses different skills than Holmes. Both stand out more clearly as individuals by comparison to one another. Their interaction as companions brings out the particulars of each in ways that their activities alone might not portray as vividly.

When first introduced, we might think of Ruth and Orpah as female Moabite counterparts to Mahlon and Chilion. The latter are brothers and paired in life and death. Their wives are not siblings but, rather, sisters-in-law. In the history of interpreting the book, some commentators conclude that they were sisters, but there is nothing to indicate that relationship in the narrative. Naomi addresses them as a pair and urges a common response on their part to the death of their husbands. Both daughters-in-law begin the journey with Naomi to Judah, cry with her, and even speak the same words to her (1:10). Subsequently, their actions diverge. Orpah finally accepts Naomi's advice and returns to Moab, while Ruth clings to her and vows to stay with Naomi, even unto death. Indeed, Ruth's vow contains an oath, a self-imprecation that the Lord would deal severely with her, should even death separate them (1:16–17).

How do we assess Orpah? To begin with, we ask about Naomi's words to her and Ruth. Naomi urges them to stay in their homeland, initially with their own mothers, and offers hope that the Lord will deal kindly with them, as they have done to her and her dead sons. In a patriarchal, pre-industrial culture, women of marriageable age find more security with a husband, and security is what Naomi says that she wants for them. Her words do not assume a legal or customary obligation of a widowed daughter-in-law to a widowed mother-in-law, nor do surviving legal codes from the ANE. One can read Naomi's dialogue differently and more manipulatively. While grateful for the kindness she has received from them, Naomi is fearful of returning alone to Judah. Although it is her ancestral home, what awaits her there? She contrasts her circumstances with those of Ruth and Orpah. They could stay in Moab and possibly find security and support with a second husband. She, on the other hand, will not have these things because God has treated her bitterly (1:13; cf. 1:20–21). Might her words evoke sympathy or even guilt among the two people left in the world who are immediately close to her?

As with Elimelech and his sons, there is no explicit evaluative word to define Orpah, and readers must do their best to interpret her from the way in which she is framed and described. She and Ruth represent two consequential choices, whatever moral, psychological, or theological profile is attributed to them. They are defined narratively by their choices. Ruth becomes an essential cog in the story of Ephrathite Bethlehem and a contributor to Judah and Israel's national history. Regarding their choices, the narrator tersely put it, "Orpah kissed her mother-in-law [and left], but Ruth clung to her" (1:14). More expansively, Orpah "went back to her people and her deities," whereas Ruth made Naomi's people, "her people" and Naomi's deity, "her God" (1:15–16). What Naomi wishes for both women—that the Lord grant them security in the house of a husband—surprisingly comes to pass with Ruth. Orpah exits the story. Period.

Ruth and Naomi are paired from the beginning to the end of the narrative, albeit in various ways. One of the marks of the narrative is the exchange between the two in dialogue. We've already given some consideration to the exchanges between the two along the road to Judah. The others take place in Bethlehem. Given the terseness of the narrative, readers are provided no indication of where the two of them live except that it is "in town" (2:18). One contrast between the two women is movement. Ruth is a doer and Naomi is a talker. Ruth is out from the domicile, gleaning during barley and wheat harvests, and visiting a threshing floor at night. These are risky endeavors for a single woman, as the narrative indicates (2:15–22, 3:14). Naomi never leaves the house, narratively speaking, during the weeks of harvest and threshing. Modern readers might be inclined to say that Naomi was depressed, but the narrator typically offers no description of her state of mind. She is rendered through her speaking and actions.

Both women initiate actions with significant repercussions in the narrative. Here are two of them. Ruth proposes to Naomi that she glean for barley and wheat during the harvest season. Her reasoning is thick with meaning: She hopes to find favor in someone's sight (2:2). In gleaning—picking up dropped stalks of grain in someone else's field—Ruth could accumulate the staple ingredient for baking bread. This would be the best time of the year in which to acquire it. She could do it with manual labor and not have to purchase or trade for it. At the same time, as a single woman she could be considered a nuisance or worse (a thief or prostitute), pushed away by owners or their workers, or even assaulted by them. This is a natural context for the comment that she would find favor in someone's eyes. She would be allowed to glean in safety. The narrator introduces the setting of Ruth's proposal to Naomi with the report that

Boaz, a kinsman of Elimelech, is a recognized member of the community. Here is another aspect of Ruth's proposal. Readers can anticipate what might transpire when meeting Elimelech's relative. Do we smile and attribute multiple meanings to Ruth's motivation or do we smile at the omniscience of the narrator to see ahead of Ruth's goal of acquiring food (cf. 2:3, 13)?

Naomi's desire that Ruth find "security" in the home of a husband is expressed again in the narrative (3:1–4; cf. 1:9), after Naomi observes the way in which Boaz assisted Ruth during the harvest season. Naomi proposes that Ruth wash, perfume herself, change clothes, and visit Boaz in the evening at a threshing floor. Once she removes his cover, Naomi asserts, Boaz will "tell you what to do." A modern storyteller might explicitly describe Naomi as calculating or manipulative, and we would still have to decide whether her motives were in Ruth's best interest or whether her push for Ruth's marriage to her kinsman was motivated primarily by her own desire for improved security status. Rather than defining further Naomi's interests, the narrator masterfully situates the mystery of mixed motives in the dialogue itself, while also presenting Ruth as a determined agent of Naomi's scheme. In a marvelous reversal, Ruth tells the befuddled Boaz what she wants—namely, that he marry her and become the kinsman-redeemer for the line of Elimelech and its surviving members (3:9).

Boaz and Mr. So-and-so are paired as family members and potential kinsmen-redeemers. They are also contrasted in the narrative by their respective choices. As noted previously, the narrative is not precise on how Boaz is related to Elimelech or to Mr. So-and-so. It is unlikely that either is a brother of Elimelech. In an indistinct phrase, Mr. So-and-so is described as closer to Elimelech than Boaz (3:12). Strangely, the kinsman is unnamed, unlike Orpah, the counterpart to Ruth. Boaz recognizes immediately that Ruth's request requires family business transactions and he moves immediately to initiate them according to clan custom. Conservative land tenure practices are in play, which make it difficult to alienate the field in question from the larger family (cf. Num. 27:1–11, 36:1–12). As noted in the previous chapter, this matter is best explained through an exploration of the cultural world behind the text and matters of property ownership in ancient Israel. The question the narrative answers clearly is which eligible family member will redeem the property.

Mr. So-and-so initially sees a good opportunity to add a field to his possession and thus commits to its purchase. He does not have to bid or compete to acquire the field. It will cost him to redeem it, but once the debt is paid, it would be his, free and clear. In terms of the plot, his problem is Ruth, the widow of Mahlon, who is of childbearing age. Boaz skillfully notes that with Elimelech's property also comes the widow and the opportunity to "maintain the dead man's name on *his* inheritance" (4:5). Mr. So-and-so declines the purchase, recognizing the potential difficulties with marriage, conflicting loyalties at home, and a potential heir who could lay claim to the field he purchased. In this regard, he is similar to Onan, who worried about complicating his family affairs if married to Tamar (Gen. 38:9).

Like Ruth and Orpah, Boaz and Mr. So-and-so are characterized by having the same choice and by making different commitments. Redemption, by definition, costs something. On the one hand, Mr. So-and-so was willing to pay the cost of the field, but not the potential costs in family complications. On the other hand, Boaz paid the cost of the field, as well as undertook the responsibility of restoring the inheritance of dead kin. Upon first meeting Ruth, Boaz offered a blessing that she receive a reward from God for all she had done on behalf of Naomi and for coming to a people she had not previously known (2:11–12). In doing so, he foreshadows a role for himself in bringing about a blessing for the line of Elimelech, the clan of Perez, and the people of Israel.

CHARACTERIZATION AND AFFIRMATIONS OF A COMMUNITY ETHOS

Three figures are commended for their actions in the narrative. Naomi commends Ruth and Orpah for their "kindness" or "loyalty" (Heb., *hesed*) to her and to their dead husbands (1:8). Boaz twice commends Ruth for her familial commitment (2:11), also using the same term (3:10). The women of Bethlehem praise Ruth as more valuable than seven sons (4:15), for her love of Naomi.

Closely related to these commendations are the blessings uttered by various figures. In commending Ruth and Orpah, Naomi hopes that the Lord will treat them kindly and that the Lord will enable them to find security in the house of a husband (1:8–9). Her affirmation connects act to consequence, overseen by the Lord, who is addressed as the one who can bring a kind result to a loyal act. Boaz similarly hopes that the Lord will reward Ruth for her fidelity to Naomi and her new community (2:12). Naomi blesses Boaz, when she sees what Ruth brings home from gleaning (2:19–20). The latter part of her formulation is delightfully ambiguous: "Blessed be he by the LORD, whose kindness [*hesed*] has not forsaken the living or the dead!" (NRSV).

The "kindness" of which she speaks can refer to either Boaz or the Lord, or perhaps it is intentionally ambiguous. In any case, she seeks a blessing from the Lord for Boaz in return for his kindness. There is no single word in English to render the Hebrew term *hesed*, used three times in the narrative. "Kindness," "loving kindness," "steadfast love," and "loyalty" all render central aspects. It is a term that represents what is good and beneficial in a relationship, but that is not required by law or forced by circumstances. Ruth was not forced to follow Naomi to Judah in a support role nor required to approach

Boaz at the threshing floor. Boaz was not forced to see to Ruth's safety and success in gleaning nor required to redeem Elimelech's field.

The assembled witnesses in the gate offer a blessing that Ruth's future progeny "build the house of Israel" (4:11) like the tribal ancestors of old. This is the intersection between the story of Ruth and Boaz and that of the larger storyline of Israel.

One of the ways these various affirmations are framed is community assessment. Boaz's foreman knows who Ruth is and Boaz makes it a point to say to Ruth that he has been told all that she has done. In the threshing-floor scene, Boaz tells Ruth that "all the gate of my people" knows that she is a worthy woman (3:11). This is an idiomatic phrase and means something like "the assembly of inhabitants" or perhaps more colloquially, "everybody here knows." It is worth noting Boaz's literal phrase, however, since it is "all the people at the gate" (4:11) who affirm Ruth's place in building up the house of Israel. Moreover, Boaz's affirmation of Ruth as "worthy" (*hayil*) is the same term the narrator used to describe Boaz in 2:1.[2] He is a person of substance, understood in material terms and in a communal assessment of his integrity. A needy gleaner in his field found favor in his eyes. Whereas Ruth does not possess much by the way of material goods, Boaz understands that her risky trip to the threshing floor and her surprising marriage proposal reflect Ruth's *hesed*—her worthy commitments to familial integrity.

We might think of community assessment in the narrative in a second, related way. The affirmations of Ruth and Boaz reflect a positive community ethos in action. It takes the exercise of *hesed* and commitment to the clan for the larger health of the community to be realized. In the commitments of Ruth and Boaz, the narrator portrays an Israelite community ethos. It is explanation and persuasion artfully at work.

THE CHARACTER OF GOD

In literary terms, God is a character in the narrative, although without a direct speaking role. In most instances, Yahweh (*YHWH*, translated as "Lord"), the personal name of Israel's God, is used. The epithet *Shaddai* ("Almighty") occurs once, along with three occurrences of *Elohim*, the generic term for deity or deities (1:15–16, 21). The narrator reports that Naomi returned to Judah after hearing that the "Lord had taken notice of his people and given them food" (1:6). Possibly, the narrator's comment that Ruth "happened" to show up in Boaz's field (2:3) is a subtle reference to divine providence. A clear statement of divine activity comes in the report that the Lord enabled Ruth to conceive (4:13). Here is the best example in the book of the authoritative narrator, who knows what God is doing in the story. Otherwise, God is rendered through the speech of human beings.

Naomi asserts that the Lord has afflicted her through the death of her husband and sons (1:13, 20–21). It reflects the belief that Naomi's life is part of the Lord's purview and actions. Her words are similar to the laments of the Psalms, where suffering and injury can be attributed to the strange work of the Lord. On occasion, the psalmist confesses sinfulness and asks for forgiveness, but the majority voices of the laments set out the incongruence of their suffering before the Lord. Naomi is bitter, not contrite, and she attributes her emptiness to the hand of the Lord. To pick up on a previous discussion, the narrative offers no explicit reason for the death of Naomi's family and it sits as a tragic event at the beginning of the story.

Naomi, nevertheless, seeks security and blessing from the Lord for her daughters-in-law, a desire she expresses repeatedly in the case of Ruth. If the Lord has been harsh with her, perhaps the Lord will treat them favorably, the way that they have treated her. This reflects an Israelite community ethos: hope that the Lord will bring kind actions back to the perpetrators. That would be one way to define the term "blessing," used several times in the narrative.

The Lord is invoked in what can be considered conventional piety. Consider the greetings between Boaz and the reapers, where he says "the Lord be with you" and they reply, "the Lord bless you" (2:4). Yet, as the narrative unfolds, "blessing" is what Boaz will give and receive. Naomi will exclaim it (2:19–20) and the people of Bethlehem will expound upon it. We might also see Boaz's invoking the Lord to Ruth as conventional piety: may the Lord reward you for your deeds (2:12). The sentiment is, after all, part of what we have called an Israelite community ethos. But what follows is worthy of note. Boaz describes Ruth as taking refuge under the wings of the Lord, the God of Israel. It is a metaphor for security and divine character, and the image is portrayed in the threshing-floor scene, where Ruth asks Boaz to spread his garment (literally "wing"; 3:9) over her. It is a request that, narratively speaking, humanly embodies the Lord's protective wings for a family in need. It portends fulfillment of the reward and blessing enunciated by both Naomi and Boaz.

And there may be more for the implied audience and the discerning modern reader. If one asks the literary question, Who else in the HB speaks of the protection of the Lord's wings?, the answer is that the metaphor occurs six times in the psalms (Ps. 17:8, 36:8, 57:1, 61:4, 63:7, 91:4). According to the secondary headings of all but one of these psalms, they represent the liturgical voice of David. It may be that Boaz's affirmation of Ruth is essentially conventional piety, and that the congruence between him and the David of the psalms is coincidence, but it is also possible that Boaz speaks of the Lord like his illustrious descendant because (literarily speaking) it is the Davidic family's testimony on display in the Ruth narrative.

The Lord uses a variety of surprising figures to build the house of Israel. The Ruth narrative is one version of that larger story, with fascinating characters to go along with the ancestral portraits in the book of Genesis and the stories of David in Samuel, Kings, and Chronicles.

IS RUTH'S STORY A LOVE STORY?

In modern Western culture, stories about marriage typically have a romance factor to them. That is an influential part of the world in front of the text for many current readers. Is romance a part of the portrayal of Ruth and Boaz? If so, it is implicit in the portrayal. Physical attraction is another important and related aspect of modern culture. The narrative offers no clues as to the appearance of Ruth and Boaz, or any of the characters for that matter. A modern novel or movie would make their appearance integral to their representation and to their emotional connection/physical attraction to one another. A glance at two movies based on the biblical book confirms these matters. They are *The Story of Ruth* (1960) and *The Book of Ruth* (2010). The only physical clues given in the biblical text are that Ruth is of childbearing age and that Boaz is probably older than she (3:10). Would it make any difference to the biblical narrative if Ruth had acne scarring on her face and was missing several teeth, or if Boaz was bald, with limited eyesight, and had two wives at home?

Perhaps we should be wary of dismissing a romantic element to the narrative or an entertainment factor in its presentation. The threshing-floor scene certainly has expectant elements to it, and the literary conventions of the day may have negated more direct characterization of sexual attraction. In any case, the narrative does employ the terminology of love: the Bethlehem women affirm that Ruth "loves" Naomi (4:15). So in more than one way, we might affirm that the book of Ruth contains a love story, depending on how we define love and how we find it portrayed in the choices made by the book's characters.

5

Narrative Art

Words and Their Meaning

TEXTS ARE LIKE CUT DIAMONDS, shaped to share their brilliance. Presenters of narratives are artists at work, including (as we have noted repeatedly) the ways they say what they communicate. Semantics, broadly defined, is the modern study of meaning expressed in linguistic form: how words communicate. Syntax, broadly defined, has to do with how words are put together in communication and sentences are structured. For our purpose of basic narrative analysis, let's think of words in context, how presenters use them, and how hearers/readers respond.

Consider, for example, Lawrence Peter Berra (1925–2015), one the best professional baseball players in the history of the game. Better known by his nickname Yogi, Berra had a penchant for colorful and sometimes confusing comments in a long public life. He was an entertaining figure, who collected his life experiences in a couple of books. Many people have adopted his humorous "wisdom" in recent decades, even if they do not know the original context or even the validity of what they attribute to him. Sayings known as "Yogi-isms" and anecdotes attributed to him abound on social media and the internet, only some of which can be documented in his lifetime.

"It ain't over till it's over." Yogi said this in the 1973 baseball season, when his team (the New York Mets) was several games out of first place in its division. It seemed improbable that the Mets would win enough of the remaining games and that the top-placed team would lose enough of its remaining games for his team to win the division title. In context, his comment meant that the Mets should play hard and not give up on the goal of a division title until it was mathematically impossible for them to attain it. In fact, his team did have a strong finish and win the division title. His aphorism appealed to the popular imagination and it has been applied countless times since in situations where a probable outcome is nevertheless undetermined and human effort and luck may yet alter the expected conclusion. Apart from an application to a context, the logic of the saying is unclear, if not quizzical!

It is not just what Yogi said but also how he said it. His use of "ain't" and contracted forms of speech reflect colloquial expression and what might be called homespun wisdom. Let's take a second example of his sayings: "It's like déjà vu all over again." The French phrase *déjà vu* refers to something already seen, and it has been adopted into English-speaking circles to refer to an event or experience similar to one encountered previously. Berra's comment came in the context of watching two baseball players hit homeruns, one after the other. Was it a mangled redundancy or perhaps a brilliant play on the phrase, where two figures are repeating the same act? His humorous adaptation of the French phrase has resulted in his aphorism being widely quoted in the United States, at times with the lead-in, "as Yogi Berra said. . . ." This saying is like several others of his, which represent his humor and odd phraseology (syntax). Note how the two sayings are syntactically similar:

It is not over until it is over.
It is déjà vu all over again.

The adopting of a French phrase into English and the ways in which it has taken root are an interesting study in semantics. Context is crucial for exploring the meaning of words and what is known of the history of their use, whether we are thinking of the French phrase *déjà vu* in an English context or the way Judah compared Tamar's "righteousness" (*sedaqah*) to his own in the family matter of an heir for his family. Of course, what is preserved about the history of a word's usage varies from culture to culture. As modern readers, we are privileged to consult a dictionary for a list of meanings for a word or phrase. Nevertheless, their employment in context is the primary way we learn what they mean in that instance. What can be known about the writer, the implied audience, the literary and historical-cultural contexts, and the assumptions of readers also contribute to the discernment of words and their meaning.

Let's go back once more to Yogi Berra and the art of expression. Perusal of some Yogi-isms (a saying or an anecdote) contributes to his characterization in our minds. And his characterization, in turn, influences how we read them and similarities to them. So, when introduced to a new Yogi-ism or story about him, we might conclude that it does sound like something Yogi would say and do. It might share terminology with previously known Yogi-isms or the strange syntax he sometimes employed. It is also probable that people who enjoyed his humor produced some "Yogi-isms" to express what is their take on the world. "Imitation is the sincerest form of flattery" goes the old proverb. Words reflect in various ways on their users.

On a broad level, readers recognize that people and narratives about them often have characteristic ways of expression. We might call it style or rhetoric or favored terminology, whether of speakers or their narrative presenters. It is likely, for example, that the narratives about Jeremiah preserve things he said and did, but it is the presenter of the book who has a hand in shaping those accounts. In analyzing a scene in the *Iliad*, interpreters might speak of what they regard as typical Homeric style. That comment assumes familiarity with the rest of the *Iliad*. One might comment on the ways in which Herodotus characteristically describes military campaigns. That analysis might be sharpened by contrasting Herodotus with what Thucydides does in his presentations. Both wrote historical narrative in classical Greek and were born only twenty-four years apart. How they use the Greek language differently or similarly can assist in understanding their respective works. On a more particular level, we may pause to consider a word or phrase in a narrative. Perhaps we encounter them for the first time or find them puzzling in this context and we are looking to understand them. A first place to look is for other instances of this vocabulary in the narrative or, if possible, in similar works. The further we are from the narrator and his or her cultural setting, the more careful we must be. At other times, we recognize that certain words or phrases are characteristic of the narrative in question, and in comparing their occurrences, we use them to make connections in the story as a whole. We have seen some examples of this in previous chapters.

WORDS REPRESENT STYLE AND SUBSTANCE

In chapter 1, we noted some characteristics of narrative style in the HB. For example, on a broad level we can speak of things like Deuteronomistic style—something characteristic of Deuteronomy and seen in varying degrees in the Former Prophets and the prose sections of the book of Jeremiah. We will look here at a text in 2 Samuel that has Deuteronomistic characteristics. Complicated questions emerge from this example. Are we referring to a distinct school of thought or an original group of writers? Did the writers have followers who kept the vocabulary, syntax, and related concerns alive for a period of time, or were there people, like the admirers of Yogi Berra, who adopted similar manners of expression without any personal contact with him? We don't have to answer these questions definitively to recognize the influence of Deuteronomistic vocabulary and thought on portions of the HB.

Another broad characteristic is wordplay in Hebrew narrative. We noted several examples already in previous discussion. Wordplay is common in classical Hebrew literature and occurs in several related forms. Interpreters, therefore, comment that particular types of wordplay are characteristic of, say, Jonah or Ruth. Repetition, a general stylistic trait in biblical narrative, is also at work in several forms of wordplay.

EXAMINING SOME WORDS AND PHRASES IN GENESIS 16 AND 38

We'll begin with the repeated phrase "to go in to" in Genesis 16:2 and 4. Sarai urges Abram, "go in to my slave." The reason she gives for this instruction (in order "to obtain children") strongly implies that the act of a man "going in to" a woman refers to sexual intercourse, something confirmed by the narrator's report that she gave Hagar to Abram "as a wife" and that he "went in to" Hagar and she conceived (16:3–4). Apart from the context, a comment that a man went in to a woman might be an odd way to say that he visited at her home or tent. Indeed, the act of entering a house or tent is possibly the origin of the term. While modern English has multiple phrases for sexual intercourse, "going in to" is not a common one for it. The only modern Western readers who might recognize the phrase as indicating sexual intercourse are those who are already familiar with it from the HB.

The phrase in Genesis 16 has a common verb ("go"), used over two thousand times in the HB for various activities. One can consult a classical Hebrew dictionary for the verb *bo'* or a detailed article on marriage in ancient Israel and learn that the phrase is used several times in the HB to refer to sexual intercourse. It is used, for example, to describe Onan and Judah with Tamar in Genesis 38:8–9 and 16, and Boaz with Ruth in Ruth 4:13.

We noted previously the wordplay on the name Ishmael in Genesis 16:11. Hagar's son will be called "God hears" because the Lord has "heard" her affliction and responded by giving her a famous son. The wordplay is on the Hebrew verb "to hear" (*sham'a*). How might we interpret this wordplay in context? Let's explore briefly two responses among several options. First, we might start with the recognition that this is one example of a larger pattern or literary motif in the ancestral stories in Genesis. More specifically, there are several other examples of wordplays for children's names in birth accounts. They occur in birth stories of eponymous ancestors—that is, ancestors whose names are later used for a people group or nation of their descendants. Here is a partial list of figures in Genesis who fit this description. One will see immediately that Ishmael is one figure in a significant list of people and tribal entities, all related to Abraham and thus to the Israelite nation:

Ishmael
Ammon
Moab
Isaac
Esau
Jacob
Reuben
Simeon
Levi
Judah

Dan
Naphtali
Gad
Asher
Issachar
Zebulun
Joseph
Benjamin

The last twelve personal names are also the sons of Jacob/Israel, the eponymous ancestors of tribal entities in the Israelite polity. The nation of Israel, or a portion thereof, could also be called Isaac, Jacob, or Joseph. Esau is more complicated, but follows the pattern. At birth he came out with red ('admoni) body hair, so he was called Esau (Gen. 25:25). The name of his putative descendants, "Edomites" (Gen. 36:1), is linked to the word for "red." Ammon and Moab, like the Edomites, are national groups located to the east of the Israelite tribal inheritances. The Ishmaelites were a mobile tribal society located to the east and south of these states.

A second response to the wordplay on Ishmael's name is to look elsewhere in the ancestral stories to see whether the verb sam'a ("hear") is used with regard to Ishmael. The parallel narrative in Genesis 21:8–21 stands out immediately. In this account Hagar's son is not named, but we are twice told that God "heard" the voice of the boy (v. 17) in their troubles and that God will make a great nation of him. His identity receives verbal reinforcement, even when he is not named.

In previous discussion of Genesis 38, we noted the function and background of the phrase "perform the duty of a brother-in-law" (v. 8), so influential to the account. It is another of the phrases that an ancient Israelite would recognize, while modern readers likely would not. Fortunately, the terminology occurs elsewhere in the HB and readers can follow the plot with more understanding. The account also has several naming wordplays.

We recognize, therefore, that the vocabulary in them shapes portions of the narrative. Er, for example, is "evil" (*ra'*) and is dealt with as such. Perez ("breach" or "breaking forth") moves swiftly through the birth canal to emerge as firstborn.

There is other repetitive vocabulary in the account. Note, for example, the multiple references to "prostitution" (vv. 15, 21–22, 24) and to the garments of widowhood. In what sense is Tamar a prostitute? She engaged in sexual relations with her father-in-law, but she received no payment. She puts on and then takes off a veil that marks her as a potential prostitute, just as she puts off and on her widow's garments, since the latter mark her status in the community. Here the repetition of clothing changes points to her shifting identities in the family dilemma.

Judah's signet, cord and staff (vv. 18, 25) are his "pledge" to pay Tamar. He would not give her to Shelah, his remaining son, to carry out the task of raising offspring for the deceased, but he was scrupulous about payment for prostitution. When Tamar absconded with his pledged identity markers, Judah remarks to his companion, "let her keep them as her own" (v. 23). When Tamar is brought before a family tribunal for prostitution, she produces the signet, cord, and staff to identify the male who impregnated her. In some sense, Judah's family identity did reside with her, since she took the initiative to reverse her widowhood and to provide an heir for Judah.

2 SAMUEL 7

This chapter plays a central role in the plotline of 1 and 2 Samuel. Here is a basic outline of it:

  I. David at rest from his enemies   7:1
  II. David contrasts his house with God's lack of a
      house   7:2

III. The prophet Nathan encourages David to act   7:3
IV. A nocturnal revelation from the Lord to Nathan   7:4–16
    A. No need for David to build a house for the Lord   7:4–7
    B. The Lord appointed David over Israel   7:8–11a
    C. The Lord will build David a house   7:11a–12
    D. David's offspring will build the Lord a house   7:13
    E. The Lord will be Father to David's offspring   7:14–15
    F. David's house and kingdom made secure   7:16
V. David's prayer in response   7:18–29

The chapter is mostly dialogue and reported speech, with a few guiding comments from the narrator (vv. 1, 4, 17). The outline follows the change in speakers and expands on the contents of Nathan's oracle, a "vision" report (v. 17). One could also expand aspects of David's prayer to the Lord, picking up other thematic elements in the chapter and the Samuel narrative. After the narrator sets the context in verse 1, the exchange goes as follows: David speaks, Nathan responds briefly, Nathan responds again after a nocturnal revelation, and David prays to the Lord in response to Nathan's oracle. The outline's expansion of Nathan's oracle puts the repetition of the term "house" before the reader, a word used fifteen times in the chapter and clearly emphasized in it.

Before looking more closely at 2 Samuel 7, let's explore some meanings of the Hebrew word for house (*bayit*). We'll summarize data readily available in a Bible dictionary. The word can have several meanings: "domicile," "palace," "household," "family," and "temple," among others. Consider, for example, the commandment not to covet a neighbor's "house" (Exod. 20:17; Deut. 5:21). The house in question may well be a physical structure, but the term likely represents what we call a household. Note that the neighbor's wife, slave, field, and animal are part of the house. In the ANE, such things were considered part of a male's household. Recall that the inhabitants of Bethlehem told Boaz that they hoped the woman coming into his *house* would be like earlier women who built the *house* of Israel, and that with children, his *house* would be like the *house* of his ancestor Perez (Ruth 4:11–12). The term *bayit* is used in multiple, related senses in this blessing. Boaz has a household (people and possessions). His extended family, what we might think of as a clan, is named the house of Perez.

According to 2 Samuel 3:1ff., there was protracted struggle between the "house of David" and the "house of Saul," in which David's extended family/clan eventually prevailed. The "house of Saul" refers not just to his Benjaminite clan but also to its status as the governing institution for Israelite tribes. David's house would have this duality as well, first for Judah and then for Israel (2 Sam. 5:5). The descendants of the ancestor Israel are also characterized as a house, defining a multitribal confederation with a kinship term (see later).

In the ANE, the house or representative dwelling for monarchs and deities can be called a *bayit*. In the case of an earthly monarch, we can use the term "palace," and in the case of a deity, we use the term "temple" or "sanctuary." The term *bayit* can be joined syntactically with another noun to form a phrase showing connection or relationship between the two nouns. The phrases "house of Israel" and "house of Perez" are two examples. The "of" is a way in English to designate the connection of the two nouns in Hebrew. When the Israelite Ark is captured by the Philistines, they bring it "into the house of Dagon and set it beside Dagon" (1 Sam. 5:2). A statue or some physical representation of Dagon was in the temple (*bayit*) that bore his name.

In 2 Samuel 7:1, the narrator informs us that the Lord had given David "rest" from his enemies and that David dwelt in his house (palace). This comment connects with the plot of 1 and 2 Samuel, which presents the rise of monarchy in Israel and how David and his family came to rule the tribes of Israel from his palace in Jerusalem. David's "rest" follows on his anointing as king over Judah and the other tribes of Israel, his capture of Jerusalem, his building of a palace there with the assistance of King Hiram of Tyre, his defeat of the Philistines, and his bringing of the sacred Ark of the Covenant into Jerusalem (2 Sam. 5–6). The Ark is a visible reminder of the presence of the Lord with the people of Israel, and David set it in a tent in Jerusalem. It would be placed in the holy of holies of the Jerusalem temple.

David tells Nathan, a prophet introduced in the Samuel narratives, that he is now living in a house of cedar, but the Ark is in a tent. A palace of cedar is a grand structure for an earthly ruler like David or a cosmic ruler like the Lord (1 Kings 5:7–12). Human builders of temples in the ANE needed divine confirmation before proceeding, and Nathan understands David's comment to be a query whether the Lord would confirm a plan to build a temple. The prophet at a royal court was a figure tasked with discerning the divine will. Note, for example, the conversation of the kings of Israel and Judah with prophets as they deliberate going to war against the Aramaeans (1 Kings 22:1–28).

Nathan's initial encouragement to David is countermanded by a nocturnal vision from the Lord. The Lord rehearses portions of the national storyline now contained in the Pentateuch and Former Prophets. This is another example of an individual story in the HB and how it intersects with the larger storyline of Israel. The contrast that David drew between his palace and a tent for the Ark is put in the context of the Lord's bringing his people from Egypt and moving about with them until they reach their appointed place in Canaan. The Ark, which represented the presence of Lord, was in a tent or tabernacle for years and not once did the Lord seek a house (temple) "to live in."

"The Lord will make a house for David" (7:11). This is a classic wordplay on *bayit*, presupposing the initial exchange between David and Nathan, and defining the Lord's future care for the people through a commitment to David's house. David's offspring, who will succeed David as ruler over Israel, will build a house for the Lord. In the continuation of the national storyline, David's son Solomon will build a temple for the Lord in Jerusalem and place the Ark of the Covenant in it. The house that the Lord will make, however, is David's family as the dynasty of rule over Israel. Note the repetition of royal language in Nathan's oracle:

> I will establish his [David's offspring] kingdom (v. 12)
>
> I will establish the throne of his kingdom forever (v. 13)
>
> Your house and your kingdom will be made sure before me,[1] your throne established forever (v. 16)

In the ANE, monarchs sit on a throne. The Davidic dynasty had one in the royal palace complex. The "house of David" can also refer to Israel under the rule of the Davidic dynasty, hence the multiple references to "kingdom." This, too, is in accord with ANE practice. Some polities (tribal associations or states) bore the name of the ruler or that of the founder of the dynasty. Note the report that the "house of David" heard of an opposing political coalition, causing a trembling heart for the Davidic king and people alike (Isa. 7:2). Indeed, the phrase "house of David" survives in a fragmentary Aramaic inscription from the ninth century BCE and probably in a Moabite inscription of a similar date. In both instances, they appear to be references by foreign kings to the state of Judah.[2]

We can follow the wordplay in David's prayer of response. It is narrative repetition at work. David prays that the Lord will confirm the word spoken about him and the promise to "build a house" for him (v. 27). David's quote actually uses a different verb than Nathan's, who reported that the Lord would "make" a house for David. There is little semantic difference between the two verbs in this instance, although we will look later at the specific phrase "to build a house" with regard to David's family. In this context, the verb "build" contributes to the wordplay on *bayit*. David's offspring will "build" a temple for the Lord, while the Lord "builds" a family kingdom for him.

In following the repetition of the term *bayit* in the narrative, and taking note of the terminology associated with it, readers construct a partial semantic field for the term. David's house is initially defined by a physical structure of cedar over against a tent, analogous to the structure that Solomon will later build for the Lord, moving the Ark from a tent and placing it in the temple. In other contexts, the term *bayit* might define the household of tent dwellers, but not here. Words like "offspring," "throne," and "kingdom" provide nuance and specificity to portray the dynastic house of David that the Lord will build.

EXPLORING SOME OTHER TERMINOLOGY IN 2 SAMUEL 7

The noun "name" occurs five times in the chapter. Like the word *bayit*, the noun *shem* is a common Hebrew term with a broad range of meaning. We can put the five occurrences of the term next to each other to begin our exploration:

> I will make a <u>great</u> *name* for you [David], like the *name* of <u>great</u> people in the land (v. 9)

> He [David's offspring] will build a house for my *name* (v. 13)

> Who is like your people Israel, the one nation that God went to redeem for himself as a people and to make for himself a *name* . . . (v. 23)

> Your *name* [Lord] will be made <u>great</u> forever, saying "the Lord of Hosts is God over Israel," and the house of your servant David will be established before you (v. 26)

A personal name represents identity. We have seen that in naming wordplays from other contexts. References to God's name (*shem*) also abound in the HB. An exclamation from temple worship such as, "I will make a thanksgiving offering to you and will call on the name of the Lord" (Ps. 116:17), shows how deeply connected "name" is to the Lord's identity in ancient Israel. To call on the name of the Lord may seem redundant syntactically to an English speaker, with no difference in meaning from "calling on the Lord." But the frequent invoking of Yahweh's "name" in the HB makes the noun almost an independent representation of the Lord (see later).

In 2 Samuel 7, "name" represents renown and reputation for the name bearers. The translations just given also show the repetition of the Hebrew term *gadal* and its cognates in portraying a name—a term whose basic meanings are to be large or to make great. In verse 9, the term is used twice as an adjective (a "great" name and "great" people). In verse 26, *gadal* is a verb and is often translated as "magnify" when praising the name of an individual. Compare the verb's use in 7:22: "you are *great*, O Lord, for there is no one like you." The actions of the Lord and that of David and his house mutually reinforce the greatness of their respective names.

There are several references elsewhere in the HB to making someone's name great, confirming the cultural and religious significance of the phrases in 2 Samuel 7. In chapter 2, we saw one of them in the words of the Lord to Abram and Sarai (Gen. 12:1–3), a text central to the theme of Genesis. But what about the phrase "a house for my name" (7:13)? This question brings us back to the discussion of *bayit*, but from the perspective of the modifying phrase "for my name." One clue comes from

Solomon's words and prayers at the dedication of the temple in Jerusalem (1 Kings 8:14–53). The king explicitly takes up the terminology of Nathan's oracle in 2 Samuel 7:5–16. If one places the two texts side by side, the connection between them is clear. Solomon claims that he "built the house for the name of the Lord, the God of Israel" (vv. 20–21; cf. 1 Kings 5:5).

In Solomon's prayer, God dwells in heaven (1 Kings 8:30, 43), while his "name" is associated with the temple in Jerusalem (8:29, 43–44, 48). As noted previously, the temple in Jerusalem can be referred to as the "house of the Lord," like the Philistine sanctuary known as the "house of Dagon"; but unlike the Philistine temple, the house in Jerusalem had no statue of the Lord. What we might call a "name theology" indicates God's ownership of the temple and immanence there for worshipers through the invisible presence of his name. Modern readers will recognize the issue at hand. Cultures wrestle with ways to present the divine world as both immanent and transcendent. The "name theology" is one formulation of this conceptual issue. The HB presents various affirmations that the Lord dwells in the temple, including those without qualification or explicit mention of the Lord's name (e.g., Ps. 132).

Solomon also quotes a revelation from God in his prayer: "your eyes may be open . . . toward this house, the place of which you said, 'my name shall be there'" (1 Kings 8:29). The quote "my name shall be there" is not reproduced verbatim elsewhere in the HB, but its substance occurs in the book of Deuteronomy, which indicates that the Lord will choose a place from among the tribes of Israel "as his habitation/dwelling, to put his name there" (Deut. 12:5; cf. 12:11). This will happen when God gives Israel "rest" from their enemies (12:10; cf. 2 Sam. 7:1, 10–11). The "place" is not further identified, but it will be a place of pilgrimage for Israelites where they can worship the Lord. Nathan's oracle is rooted in this Deuteronomistic vocabulary, just as its content is further explicated through

Solomon's words at the temple's dedication. In the DtrH, Jerusalem and the temple are collectively the "place" the Lord has chosen for his name to dwell.

BUILDING A HOUSE AS PART OF THE NATIONAL STORYLINE

Nathan's oracle in 2 Samuel 7 also contains a brief presentation of Israel's story from the exodus to the rise of the Davidic monarchy in Jerusalem. That story is told in longer form in the DtrH. As part of that literary presentation, Nathan's oracle also interprets it, pointing backward to the time of judges (2 Sam. 7:11a) and forward to the establishment of the temple in Jerusalem. His oracle alludes only briefly to the accounts of struggles and national difficulties that brought David to power—accounts that constitute much of the plot in 1 Samuel 1 through 2 Samuel 3.

Let's look briefly at one statement that alludes to the larger storyline: "I will not remove my steadfast love from him [David's offspring], as I removed it from Saul, whom I removed from before you" (7:15). The translation is a bit wooden, but it shows the threefold repetition of the verb "remove" (Heb., *sur*), a repetition typically obscured in translation for stylistic reasons. More important is the reference to Saul. He and his house were the first rulers over the tribes of Israel, and the relationship between Saul and David is central to the plotline of 1 and 2 Samuel. In the narratives, Saul is both affirmed by the Lord as king over Israel and rejected by the Lord as king (1 Sam. 8–16). This duality makes for interesting literary and theological analysis! Note Saul's portrayal in Nathan's statement. The phrase "steadfast love" translates the Hebrew word *hesed*. It is the same term used to describe the beneficent actions of Ruth and Boaz (cf. discussion in chapter 4). Saul had the favor and support of the Lord and then the Lord removed it. Let's set aside discussion of Saul's failures as portrayed in 1 Samuel and remain with the statement in context. The fate of King Saul looms large in the background to Nathan's oracle, peaking through explicitly only here. We might put the matter in the form of questions: Since God rejected Saul, might God reject David, too? Just how committed is God to Israel's future and to David's family?

Some readers may conclude that a pro-David perspective shapes the narratives of 1 and 2 Samuel, so that Saul and his house do not get a balanced presentation. If so, this perspective does not keep the compilers from presenting David's flaws in the last chapters of 2 Samuel (11–24), as we shall see in the next chapter. Nevertheless, one can interpret Nathan's oracle as an example of winners writing history. The house of David overcame the house of Saul, built a temple in Jerusalem, and ruled there for centuries.

Nathan's oracle portrays what God's *hesed* looks like in action, despite Saul's failures. David's enemies are defeated; he will have a great name, and his posterity will continue. God will treat David's offspring like a father with his son—discipline yes, but no rejection. And there is the repeated adverbial phrase of "forever," used to describe the establishment of kingdom and throne (vv. 13, 16). God is committed to the future of Israel, and the house of David is a means to that end.

6

Narrative Art

Words and Their Meaning, Continued

IN THE PREVIOUS CHAPTER, WE looked briefly at some of the sayings of Yogi Berra to illustrate how words and phrases are used. In what follows we want to continue this line of exploration. Let's start with an example of a newspaper article.

On April 25, 2014, the *Houston Chronicle* ran a piece by Ericka Mellon with the headline: "Young Literacy Group Gets $300,000 Leg Up." The reporter provides an account of a press conference, at which a federal agent announced a grant for a Houston-based foundation. The article begins:

> The nascent campaign to improve Houstonians' reading skills got a $300,000 kick-start Thursday from the federal agency that oversees community service. The three-year grant will fund 15 workers to assist the Barbara Bush Houston Literacy Foundation, which is spearheading a local reading improvement effort.
>
> Wendy Spencer, who leads the Corporation of National and Community Service in Washington, D.C., held up a brown cowboy boot as she announced the grant. "We are going to stamp out illiteracy and we're gonna put boots on the ground," Spencer said.

The article goes on to describe a report released by the Bush Foundation that called for the expansion of pre-kindergarten classes in Houston and described some ways in which the federal grant would assist the foundation's efforts. It was accompanied by a picture of Ms. Spencer standing at a microphone and holding up a cowboy boot.

The reporter uses clear prose (syntax) and inserts quotations from various sources for her readers. Her text is both influenced by her life setting and constrained by the sources she cites. Put another way, she chooses her words carefully to fit her genre (narrative reporting) and intended audience, using sources she has consulted.

Take, for example, the idiomatic phrase "leg up" in the headline. A native English speaker will recognize it as an expression of gaining an advantage or making progress toward an objective. Would a native English speaker three hundred years ago recognize the phrase? That depends on when it became a common English expression. What about a nonnative speaker, who may wonder initially about the role of "lifting" a leg in the foundation's work? That depends on recognizing a figure of speech from a different culture. The phrase is a good example of an expression whose meaning is reasonably clear from context, but might not be immediately understood by some. By "context" is meant the modest-sized, prose article that reports positively on additional funding for a worthy cause. Even if its literal meaning might seem strange for someone from colonial New England or, say, Luanda, Angola, where English is likely a third language, the context of the phrase could guide either one to its approximate meaning. But this example also raises the question of another meaning of context: that of the audience and what it knows.

Another example would be the verb "spearheading." It, like the previous phrase "leg up," comes from the cultural context of the reporter. Spears have been around for millennia and have broad, cross-cultural resonance. Turning the noun "spearhead" into a verb is also understandable in the context of the article, referring there to a decisive, leading effort.

Let's take a third example from the article: the phrase "boots on the ground." Ms. Spencer used it in her remarks at the press conference, and it is dutifully reported in the article. Moreover, at the press conference she held a cowboy boot in her hand, so it was clearly a carefully chosen phrase. Ms. Spencer took a phrase in current usage and applied it to a situation in Houston, a town in which the wearing of cowboy boots is a familiar occurrence. She chose a point of contact with the culture of the audience to illustrate her point. "Cowboy boots on the ground," however, is not a common phrase to describe active engagement in either Houston or the United States. In the broader American culture, "boots on the ground" has been used in recent years to describe the presence of American soldiers (wearing combat boots) on the ground in foreign countries. A search for the phrase in statements from politicians and government officials will produce hundreds of examples of its use. Perhaps the aspect of physical engagement is assumed in Ms. Spencer's words, given the prominence of the phrase in modern political discourse. Since the 1960s, various government enterprises have been involved in what a previous American president (Lyndon B. Johnson) called the "War on Poverty." By all accounts, illiteracy is a prime contributor to poverty. Ms. Spencer may well have the idea that her agency in Washington, D.C., is actively engaged in a struggle against poverty and that "boots on the ground" appropriately conveys that stance. On the other hand, it is also possible that she did not think consciously about the primary use of the common phrase, but simply adopted it as her own for the moment to celebrate increased efforts to overcome illiteracy. We should take note in this example of the difference between (a) seeking what was in the mind of the speaker and (b) asking how her intended audience would understand her words.

Writers of narratives in the HB similarly used vocabulary from their own experience, words in current usage and known to their audience, and material taken from their sources, some of which can be considerably older in origin. As readers, we are guided first by the literary context in which terms appear; second, by the ways in which the author uses the same or similar vocabulary elsewhere; and third, by the ways in which other writers use the same or similar terms. What can be known about the historical and cultural context of the time of writing is also influential for understanding. That historical context may be some distance, chronologically speaking, from the setting under portrayal in the narrative.

VOCABULARY IN CONTEXT: SOME EXAMPLES FROM THE NARRATIVE OF RUTH

According to the narrator, the whole town was stirred when Naomi and Ruth appeared (Ruth 1:19–22). "Is this Naomi?" said some of the women of Bethlehem. The question evokes an emotional response from Naomi:

> Don't call me Naomi [pleasantness] any longer; call me Mara [bitter],
> Because the Almighty has acted bitterly with me.
>
> I went away full, but the Lord brought me back empty.
> Why call me Naomi, since the Lord has testified against me;
> Indeed, the Almighty has treated me harshly.

Naomi's suggested name change and the reasons for it contain a triple wordplay. The Hebrew word *na'am* has the basic meaning of "pleasant." The first wordplay contrasts her name with the word "bitterness." The second is a play on her changed name, reinforcing its harshness in the assertion that God has treated her "bitterly." The third is another contrast by describing an earlier "full" departure and an "empty" return to Bethlehem. Her emptiness is from the Lord's testimony against her and judgment upon her.

Let's explore briefly the Hebrew term "bitter." Readers can find other examples of noun and verbal forms of the term in the HB by using a concordance, a lexicon, a dictionary, or a wordbook of Hebrew terms. The term can refer to a bitter taste (Isa. 5:20; Exod. 12:8, 15:23). And as one might anticipate, it is frequently used to describe emotions and experiences. King Hezekiah confesses that his bad health had been of great bitterness to him (Isa. 38:15, 17). Hannah, a woman without children, is described as "bitter in spirit" and weeping in prayer to the Lord (1 Sam. 1:10). Mourning for the loss of a child is an expression of bitterness (Zech. 12:10). One can see the intersection of emotion and experience in these examples, and that the term can refer to either one. With regard to actions, the verb is also used to describe harsh measures inflicted upon someone. The Egyptians treated the Hebrew slaves badly (Exod. 1:14); archers attack severely (Gen. 49:23); and an enraged king moves toward battle (Dan. 11:11).

This brief survey shows something of the semantic range of the term "bitter" and offers some pertinent background for assessing Naomi's words. In her case, she also uses the verb in Ruth 1:13 to claim that her circumstances are more bitter for her than for her daughters-in-law. As a contextual clue, this would be primary evidence for determining the meaning of the term in 1:20. Her claim in 1:13 is in the context of a "what if" discussion about her daughters-in-law waiting years for another husband, something theoretically possible for them, but not for her. Additionally, this assists readers with her "full" and "empty" contrast later in the chapter. We might be inclined to question whether she really left Bethlehem full; but in the matter of an intact family, it is an accurate statement. Similarly, she did not return to Bethlehem completely empty (she had Ruth!), but she did arrive without the husband and children with whom she left. In 1:13, she attributes this greater bitterness/vexation to the "hand of the Lord," something essentially repeated in 1:20–21. Note that "the Almighty" is the subject of the verb "bitter" in 1:20. Naomi asserts that God is the agent of her distress.

Our brief survey also begins an answer to the question: Who in Israel talks like this? It is an important question for reading the Ruth narrative. Is such an outburst typical or atypical in the literature of the HB? What cultural and religious elements are in play here? In the HB, people in distress over suffering and loss do talk like this. In the examples just cited, Hannah cried out to God at the shrine in Shiloh and Hezekiah prayed to the Lord in Jerusalem. Such language, therefore, can be associated with prayer. In the book of Psalms, a collection of hymns and prayers from the worship life of Israel, the most frequent type of prayer is what interpreters call a lament. These are prayers of individuals and of (corporate) Israel who lament and/or complain about their circumstances. They may assert their innocence in light of unjustified persecution, confess the pain that their sins have brought upon them, or otherwise lift up debilitating circumstances to the Lord. The opening poetic verses of Psalm 38 provide a helpful illustration:

> Lord, do not rebuke me on account of your anger,
> Or discipline me because of your wrath.
> Your arrows are deep in me,
> And your hand has descended upon me.
> There is no soundness in me due to your indignation,
> My bones are unhealthy on account of my sin. (vv. 1–3)

The psalm is an individual's plea for healing and restoration, a prayer that also assumes sinfulness has wreaked havoc in the psalmist's life. Note the conclusion to verse 2: the Lord's hand has come down upon the penitent. This is a phrase like that of Naomi's, where she describes her bitterness as the hand of the Lord against her (Ruth 1:13).

Psalm 6, another lament, has a very similar beginning:

Lord, do not rebuke me on account of your anger,
Or discipline me because of your wrath.
Be gracious to me, Lord, for I am weak,
Heal me for my bones quiver.
My soul is greatly shaken,
But you Lord, how long? (vv. 1–3)

In this psalm, there is no confession of sin, only shaking and consternation at terrible personal circumstances, along with grief and weeping. There is also a plea to the Lord to refrain from discipline, along with the plaintive question: How long (shall these circumstances go on)?

The HB has a book with the English title Lamentations. It consists of poetry lamenting the devastation of Jerusalem by the Babylonians in 587 BCE and the ongoing effects of that humiliation upon survivors. There are several speaking voices in the book, including personified Jerusalem. An unnamed man speaks in chapter 3, listing numerous ways in which he has felt God's judgment. At one point he confesses that God has made him "satiated with *bitterness*" (Lam. 3:15), using the noun form of the term employed by Naomi to describe God's treatment of her. The book is yet another answer to the question, who in Israel talks like this? The phenomenon of lamenting is part of Israel's cultural and religious profile, so that figures from kings to widows engage in it. They do so in addressing God as well as human contemporaries.

Our survey of "bitter" also brings us to consider Job, a primary lamenting figure in the HB. In one of his dialogues, Job asserts that "the Almighty has embittered my soul" (Job 27:2), sounding similar to Naomi. Or should we say that Naomi sounds similar to Job? If we step back and compare the two figures more broadly, we might make a case that Ruth's narrator drew upon the story of Job, given his renown as a figure from the past (Ezek. 14:14, 20) and the prominence of his laments in the book. Similarities between the works, however, are easier to demonstrate than dependence; and recognition of them is more important to a productive reading strategy. Both figures lament their circumstances in dialogue with others. Naomi does so with her daughters-in-law and the women of Bethlehem; Job does so in cycles of exchanges with his companions. In Job's case, the narrator makes it clear that Job's terrible circumstances were not the result of his sinfulness, even though his friends were convinced of it. In Naomi's case, the connection between sin and suffering is not explicit, either. Both figures are explicit that God has treated them harshly, however they connect their failures to their circumstances. This is a key connection between the portraits of Job and Naomi. And both figures also regain family members at narrative's end as a sign of God's favor, another connection between presentations. Naomi's daughter-in-law proves more valuable than seven sons and she gets a grandson who will restore her life. In his restoration, Job gets seven sons and three daughters, plus the gift of seeing four generations before he dies.

What has become clear in the investigation is that figures lamenting their circumstances, prayerfully and otherwise, are well represented in the HB. As noted, this type of literary representation is rooted in the cultural context of ancient Israel and consistent with its religious traditions, including public prayers. Figures who lament in the HB obviously use a number of terms beside "bitter" to voice their despair or anger, Naomi and Job obviously included. We intersect with this literary tradition, however, by comparing vocabulary in a particular work and proceeding from the data to see the phenomenon in a larger narrative context.

In her complaint, Naomi noted that she departed Bethlehem "full" but returned "empty" (*rayqam*). The adjective "empty" is not an opaque or frequently used term, but its two occurrences in Ruth contribute to the plot of the book in which elements of Naomi's family are restored. That restoration is intimated in the way the narrator links the two uses of the term "empty" in the story. After the dramatic encounter at the threshing floor, Ruth tells Naomi (3:17): "He [Boaz] gave me these six measures of barley, for he said 'don't go back *empty* (*rayqam*) to your mother-in-law.'"

Most modern versions render the adjective *rayqam* as "empty-handed," an understandable English translation. It does, however, obscure somewhat the connection between 1:21 and 3:17, and thus one of the ways that the narrator develops the theme of God's reversal of Naomi's emptiness.

We noted in chapter 4 that Boaz and Ruth have a common designation as a person of "substance" or "worth." The Hebrew noun is *hayil*. The narrator informs us that Boaz is a "man of substance" (Ruth 2:1) and reports that Boaz informs Ruth that the people of Bethlehem know that she is a "woman of worth" (3:11). After a brief look at the Hebrew noun, two further observations will guide our consideration this terminology. The first is that the phrase "person of substance/worth" occurs several times elsewhere in the HB, and the second is that the noun occurs a third time in the book of Ruth (4:11).

The noun *hayil* is used in several capacities in the HB. It has the general sense of power or ability. Horses, for example, have great *strength* (Ps. 33:17). Hannah acknowledges in a prayer that in dealing with God, the "bows of the strong are broken, while the weak put on *strength*" (1 Sam. 2:4). This connection of power or strength to a martial context occurs elsewhere, so that the term is sometimes translated as "army." In the account of Pharaoh's pursuit of fleeing Israelites, God gains the upper hand against Pharaoh's army (Exod. 14:4). Ezekiel can refer to the great army of another pharaoh (17:17). The term can refer generally to wealth or possessions (Job 20:18) and to the social standing that these things bring their owners (Neh. 3:34).

With this semantic range in mind, we can understand the application of the term, singly and collectively, to people. In fighting with the Philistines, King Saul looked for a "son of *hayil*" to add to the army (1 Sam. 14:52). This is a literal rendering of a phrase that means a male of substance or ability. Similarly, Moses enjoined the "sons of *hayil*" to enter the promised land (Deut. 3:18). When the son of a prominent priest came to Adonijah with an important message, David's son welcomed him as a "man of *hayil*," a phrase intended to compliment his abilities and affirm his integrity. This is the same term used of Boaz in Ruth 2:1. A productive wife is literally a "woman of *hayil*" (Prov. 12:4, 31:10). This is the same phrase used for Ruth (3:11).

Finally, men and women can "do *hayil*" (Num. 24:18; Deut. 8:18; Prov. 31:29). Here the noun in the phrase refers to the successful outcome of human effort and means something like "be successful." This phrase—"do *hayil*"—is used in Ruth 4:11.

Let's go back to the Ruth narrative in light of this brief survey. The narrator describes Boaz initially as a relative of Elimelech and a "man of *hayil*" (Ruth 2:1). This comes in the context of Boaz's visiting his property and the reapers working there for him. Here are four English translations of the phrase:

"a man of substance"	Tanakh Translation
"a man of standing"	NIV
"a prominent rich man"	NRSV
"a man of worth"	CEB

All of these are plausible renderings. From the context of the story, they all assume that *hayil* has more to do with wealth and public standing than with physical prowess or military status. This is another illustration of how words depend on contextual clues for nuance. Elimelech is a property owner, he has resources to purchase additional property, and he is likely an older man (i.e., putting him past prime military service).

And there is the matter of Boaz's description of Ruth in 3:11. It comes in the context of her request that he undertake the role of kinsman-redeemer and that he marry her. Here are four English translations of the phrase:

"a fine woman"	Tanakh Translation
"a woman of noble character"	NIV
"a worthy woman"	NRSV
"a woman of worth"	CEB

Again, these are plausible renderings. She has neither his social standing nor his possessions, but she is worthy in matters of commitment to the clan. As a woman of worth or noble nature, she is rendered through a metaphorical extension of the term *hayil*. Indeed, we might find in the use of the English term "worth/worthy" a nice play on two senses of that term, reflecting something of the semantic play in the Hebrew original.

As we saw briefly in chapter 4, these two phrases interpret one another in the story of Ruth. We learn that Boaz is not only a man of material substance and social standing but also one of character and integrity. We learn that Ruth is a worthy example of commitment and integrity (as well as a risk-taker!) and that she will become a wife and mother of substance in Judah. We should note here the parallel phrases from proverbial wisdom (Prov. 12:4, 31:10) describing an excellent wife. Boaz's use of the same phrase would likely reverberate similarly in the mind of the intended audience of the book.

The townspeople offer a blessing to Boaz—that in his house Ruth would become like Rachel and Leah, who built the house of Israel, and that Boaz would "do *hayil* in Ephrathah and proclaim a name in Bethlehem." The last two clauses are purposefully rendered literally. This blessing contains the third and final use of the noun in the book of Ruth. Here are four renderings of the last two clauses in 4:11. The two clauses are poetic in formulation, mutually reinforcing each other:

"prosper in Ephrathah and proclaim   Tanak Translation
   your name in Bethlehem"
"may you have standing in Ephrathah   NIV
   and be famous in Bethlehem"
"may you produce children in Ephrathah   NRSV
   and bestow a name in Bethlehem"
"may you be fertile in Ephrathah   CEB
   and may you preserve a name in
   Bethlehem"

These translations vary considerably. Those of the NRSV and CEB see in the phrase "do *hayil*" the nuance of fertility. There are two reasons for this. One is the immediate context of the blessing—namely, that in having children Boaz and Ruth can build the house of Israel. The second is the conclusion on the part of some translators that *hayil* can have a secondary meaning of potency in reproduction and that such a sense fits well in the present context. The translations of Tanakh and NIV follow the sense of the phrase elsewhere in the HB (Num. 24:18; Deut. 8:18, 31:29), where it refers more generally to achieving wealth and standing in the community. These renderings illustrate how translators weigh options in presenting a narrative for readers.

When we compare the three uses of *hayil* in the Ruth narrative, we can see how they are a thread to draw portions of the account together in artful form. Readers encounter a man of substance, who takes a risk to marry a woman of substance, and who together with her contributes to the national storyline of Israel.

Three different characters in the book of Ruth are described as a *go'el*, often translated in English as "kinsman-redeemer." They are Boaz (2:20), Mr. So-and-so (4:1), and Obed (4:14). The drama of the narrative turns, in large measure, on the way in which Naomi and Ruth are redeemed from perilous economic and social forces. The term *go'el* is a participle/noun. The verb "redeem" (*ga'al*) is used multiple times, while a derivative noun (*ge'ullah*), referring to the right or option to redeem, occurs once (4:6). The verb and its derivatives occur twenty-two times in the book. The sheer number of occurrences are also evidence of the centrality of redemption to the story.

Who and what was a kinsman-redeemer? In brief, a kinsman-redeemer is a male family member who uses resources available to him in support of the clan. In chapter 4, we noted some of the legal and cultural aspects of a kinsman-redeemer, particularly as they relate to the acquisition of family property and the maintenance of family identity. The term *go'el* has a rich semantic range. Two brief narratives illustrate the activities of a *go'el* and give us perspective on its usage in Ruth. During the difficult months of the Babylonian siege of Jerusalem, a cousin of Jeremiah named Hanamel comes to visit the prophet, who is in some form of detention, with the proposition that Jeremiah purchase property belonging to his uncle Shallum (Jer. 32:6–15). The economic circumstances for Judah during the prolonged siege of the capital city were dire, and Shallum and Hanamel were looking for resources to support their family. Think of Elimelech and his property during the famine. And as with Elimelech's property, so it was with Shallum's field; it can only be "acquired" by members of the family. As Hanamel put it to Jeremiah, buy the field in Anatoth, for you have the right of possession and "redemption" (32:8). This last term is *ge'ullah*, the same term used in Ruth 4:6 to describe the right of redemption that first accrued to Mr. So-and-so and then to Boaz. In purchasing the field Jeremiah would also redeem it—that is, keep it in the family, while assisting Shallum and Hanamel with their difficult economic circumstances.

The second narrative presents a widow who makes an appeal to King David to save the life of her remaining son, so that her deceased husband would have the continuance of "name and descendant on the earth" (2 Sam. 14:1–24, 7). Think of Boaz marrying Ruth in order to "maintain the name of the dead on his inheritance, so that the name of the dead will not be cut off from his kin" (Ruth 4:10). The appeal of the widow to King David is a superb short account, with subterfuge and poignancy as parts of its narrative tension. She tells David that her two sons had fought, with one killing the other, with the result that her clan sought the life of the surviving son as retribution. Her initial appeal to David is that he take action to thwart the "avenger of blood," a kinsman who would act on behalf of the clan in carrying out the judgment on her son (v. 11). The term translated as *avenger* is *go'el*. "Blood" represents the life principle (Lev. 17:11). When Cain kills his brother Abel, God informs him that the "blood of your brother cries out from the ground" (Gen. 4:10). Abel's life and that of his family deserve vindication. Would it make a difference for a modern reader if the phrase "avenger of blood" was rendered "redeemer of blood" or "redeemer of a life lost"? Elsewhere in the HB, there are instructions for setting up cities of refuge, so that there might be checks and balances on the pursuit of people and resulting blood feuds (Num. 35; Josh 20). These instructions are reminders of the central roles that a *go'el* can play in clan life and the seriousness with which the loss of life, inheritance, and property are taken in it. Neither Boaz nor Obed is a *go'el* of blood, but they do maintain the life and family integrity of the living and the dead.

We might ask how the story of the redemption of Elimelech's family (for that is one way to describe the short story of Ruth) connects to the wider redemptive theme in Israel's national storyline. We offered some comments on this connection in chapter 3; here are some others. The story in Ruth is clearly shaped by Israel's Primary History, as the references in it to the ancestors and to David make clear. At the center of the Primary History is the account of God's rescue of the Israelite slaves from Egypt (Exod. 1–15). Historians debate the historical reality of an Egyptian sojourn and departure for Israel's ancestors, but the reader of the HB cannot miss the hundreds of references to it in the biblical texts. There are, furthermore, multiple references to God as Israel's *go'el* in the HB. The question is whether the theme of redemption in Ruth is influenced by the redemption story of Israel from Egyptian slavery in the Primary History. Let's take the self-identification of God in calling Moses as a reminder (Exod. 6:5–6):

> I have heard the groaning of the Israelites whom the Egyptians hold as slaves . . . tell the Israelites, "I am the Lord; I will free you from the burdens of the Egyptians and deliver you from slavery to them. I will *redeem* [verb is *ga'al*] you with an outstretched arm. . . ."

One of the themes that runs through the Exodus narrative is that the slaves groaned or cried out to God because of their suffering (e.g., 3:7). Is the narrator's presentation of Naomi shaped by the larger motif of Israel's crying out to the Lord? In the Exodus narrative, God is the redeemer of Israel's life, putting right what they could not accomplish on their own. Does Israel's enslavement remind one Naomi and Ruth, who were bound by circumstances beyond their control? If so, was this something intended by the narrator in the attempt to explain and persuade, or is the common vocabulary simply the result of drawing on common motifs in Israelite culture? On the one hand, Naomi's lament is in response to a query from the women of Bethlehem, not a direct cry to the Lord. Boaz and Obed are the human redemptive agents for Naomi and Ruth, not the Lord defeating Pharaoh's army. On the other hand, Boaz affirmed Ruth as having come to live under the wings of the Lord (2:12) and Naomi recognized God at work in not forsaking the living or the dead (2:20). The question depends in part on what readers, ancient or contemporary, bring to their engagement with Ruth. There is nothing in the short story itself that points to the Exodus narrative, as it does to the stories in Genesis or Samuel. Yet, readers of Israel's Primary History may discern a number of intersections and shared motifs when they come to Ruth, and vice versa. Ruth and the Primary History have a family resemblance as members of the HB.

Section II

THE WORLD BEHIND THE TEXT

7

Narrative Contexts

History and Culture

DOWNTON ABBEY, A BRITISH-PRODUCED, AWARD-WINNING
television series, has been an international hit and one of the
most successful ventures in recent visual entertainment. It
concluded a sixth and final season in 2015. *Downton Abbey* was
a historical period drama depicting the lives of the Crawleys,
a fictional aristocratic family in England, during the years
1912 to 1925. The producers worked hard to depict the historical period accurately, whether through dialogue and custom
or in the intersections of the fictional family with historical
persons and events of the time. To watch an episode was to be
transported back in time and to marvel at the ways in which
certain topics were then addressed, such as women working
outside the home; or how influential events were engaged, such
as World War I; or how a historical figure such as the Prince of
Wales was portrayed. The series is an artistic masterpiece, entertaining, imaginative, and educational. It had an explanatory
function, looking at the past as a way to better understand the
human condition and the ways in which that condition can be
understood through the lens of historical presentation.

The narratives of the HB are also historical period
dramas. As with *Downton Abbey*, they present the lives of
families and nations as they intersect on a broader world
stage. Some interpreters prefer the phrase "fictionalized

historical narratives" for them, since they believe that many of the characters in them are like the Crawley family—creations of the narrator or of the sources drawn upon by the narrator. For example, the person of Noah in the book of Genesis may never have existed historically. There were, however, great floods in the Middle East in prehistoric times, and how the divine and human communities dealt with them spawned rich reflections in ANE literature, Genesis 6–9 included. A figure like Abraham is set in a geographic and cultural context known from various sources (e.g., textual, archeological), but we've no confirmation of him as a historical person outside the book of Genesis. He could be an actual figure from the Middle Bronze period (2000–1550 BCE) or a composite character comprising various traditions emerging in a literary portrait over centuries of time. Omri and Ahab were kings in Israel in the first half of the ninth century BCE and attested in extra-biblical texts. They surely qualify as historical figures in any sense of the phrase. Historians have concluded that they were two of the strongest rulers in Israelite history, but Omri's reign gets only eight verses of text in 1 Kings (16:21–28), and the longer portrait of Ahab is concerned to show his sinfulness, not his building or military prowess.[1]

The narratives of the HB are historical in the primary sense that they render a national history for their intended audience (Israel and Judah). As classic texts, they have explanatory and persuasive functions, which certainly include an imaginative entertainment factor that proceeds from artistic expression. Who said that telling a national history should be boring? These narratives refer to people, places, events, and customs, all of which contribute to the realistic sense of the narratives for the intended audience, while providing data for the tasks of historians and anthropologists. In what follows, we'll depend on two basic observations for a broad historical sense: the first is that the narratives in the HB can be interpreted in light of the time and events that are presented by the narrator; and the second is that such narratives can also be interpreted by the context in which they were composed, which may be centuries after the events narrated. If we go back once more to the example of *Downton Abbey* and its historical narrative, we see that the intended television audience is a century or more removed from the events depicted. By entering imaginatively into a past epoch, the audience hopes to understand it and the present better.

RUTH AS A HISTORICAL NARRATIVE DURING THE TIME OF THE JUDGES

In Israel's national storyline, the book of Ruth is set during the period of tribal life in Canaan before the rise of monarchy, a period described as the "days of the Judges" (1:1). One of the books of the Former Prophets bears the name Judges, and in English translations of the Bible, the book of Ruth comes right after it, as if Ruth were a continuation of the storyline of the period, but from a different hand or narrator. The name Judges comes from the noun and verb forms of the Hebrew term *shaphat*, which has the basic meaning of rule and lead. Contemporary readers will first think of a person with judicial responsibilities, but that is to read a perfectly acceptable modern meaning into an ancient term. According to the stories in the book of Judges, a judge is a person whom YHWH raised up to lead one or more of the Israelite tribes in freeing themselves from control by a neighboring force such as the Moabites or the Philistines. That person might also have prophetic characteristics or administrative tasks related to judicial matters.

The book of Judges looks back on a time in tribal history when there was no king in Israel. Indeed, that very phrase "there was no king in Israel" occurs four times in the book of Judges (17:6, 18:1, 19:1, 21:25). Interpreters recognize that the book of Judges was compiled after kingship had taken institutional form in Israel and that the presentation of the period of the Judges in the book is shaped by the later experience of monarchy. We could have an interesting discussion about the question: "Do the compilers of the book of Judges think that the Israelite tribes were better or worse off than when indigenous monarchy arose to govern them?" In any case, later Israelites described a segment of earlier history as the period of Judges (leaders and deliverers), a time different from that of monarchical rule. On the one hand, many of the traditions in Judges come from the pre-monarchic period. On the other hand, the book did not reach its final form until centuries after the period it depicts. The book refers, for example, to the time that "the land went into captivity" (Judg. 18:30), which in context refers to the Assyrian conquests in the years 734–720 BCE.

The book of Judges contains a number of chronological references to periods of oppression and peace (e.g., 3:14, 30). If added together, they equal some four hundred years. Most interpreters, however, have concluded that at least some of the events in the book overlapped and that the period of the Judges was more likely a couple of centuries or so in duration. They often use the term "pre-monarchical" to describe it. Kingship emerged in 1050 to 1000 BCE in Israel. Historians also use standard historical periods for reference points. The Late Bronze Age in Canaan is dated ca. 1550–1200 BCE and the Iron Age I is ca. 1200–950 BCE.[2]

Readers of the Ruth narrative will recognize immediately that it contains no account of a judge or of conflict with other inhabitants of Canaan. Thus the reference to the time of the Judges in 1:1 is to provide a recognized setting, a connection to the national storyline, for later readers. And while the account is shaped by various traditions from the national storyline, it is particularly influenced by the Davidic monarchy in Israel, as we have previously noted. There is an analogy with the brief description of the book of Judges given here. Ruth's narrative is set in the pre-monarchic period of tribal life, but it too is shaped by the later experience of monarchy in Israel and the subsequent national history of Judah. How much later is an interesting historical question. It could be a matter of a century or so after the establishment of the Davidic dynasty or even several centuries later. One clue comes in the narrator's comment regarding the confirmation of transactions in Israel (4:7): In "former times" one party gave his sandal to the other party in a property exchange. Although vague in terms of chronological reckoning, the narrator's "former times" explanation indicates that the intended audience existed at some cultural and historical distance from the events depicted in the narrative. Perhaps the cultural context of the intended audience typically had written deeds as part of a property exchange (cf. Jer. 32:9–15) and the narrator provided an explanatory comment for a detail contained in the tradition? We will return to this topic in the next chapter.

Words and their usage are important evidence for a historical reading of a biblical narrative. Analysts looking at texts in the HB often use the terms "Standard Biblical Hebrew" and "Late Biblical Hebrew" to describe linguistic characteristics and thereby suggest approximate dates for a text's composition. Standard Biblical Hebrew refers to the grammar, vocabulary, and syntax used in the pre-exilic period—that is, the ninth to seventh centuries BCE, while Late Biblical Hebrew refers to the same characteristics as they appear in Hebrew texts of the sixth to second centuries BCE. Put another way, Standard Biblical Hebrew is the classical Hebrew of the First Temple period and Late Biblical Hebrew is the literary Hebrew of the Second Temple period. As it turns out, interpreters have placed the composition of Ruth at more than one place along this linguistic timeline. On the one hand, the grammar and syntax have much in common with Standard Biblical Hebrew, yet there are elements in it, such as an occasional Aramaic term, that may represent an exilic or post-exilic setting. There are a couple of things to keep in mind in the discussion of semantics and the dating of narrative compositions. One is that the approximate dating of a composition may be more helpful for understanding the setting of the narrator and the intended audience than in dating some of the contents. Traditions and expressions can be passed along in oral and written form for centuries before final incorporation in a document. Another is that a significant amount of narrative material in the HB took shape in the eighth to fifth centuries BCE and thus will have mixed linguistic characteristics.

EHUD AND THE OPPRESSION OF MOAB (JUDGES 3:12–30)

We want to examine the brief account of one of the deliverers (judges) in the book of Judges as an exercise in historical analysis. These are primarily the What, Where, and When questions applied to the text. Ehud is a man from the tribe of Benjamin, who is instrumental in freeing Israelites from Moabite control. Here is a basic outline of the account:

    I. Israel's failure and the oppression of Eglon, king of Moab 3:12–14

    II. The Lord raises up Ehud as deliverer 3:15a

    III. Ehud presents tribute to Eglon 3:15b–18

    IV. Ehud has a message from God for Eglon 3:19–20

    V. Ehud kills Eglon and escapes 3:21–23

    VI. Eglon's servants discover his corpse 3:24–25

VII. Ehud leads successful battle against the
     Moabites   3:26–29
VIII. Moab is subdued and the land has rest   3:30

One of the interesting characteristics of the account is the relative lack of dialogue. The narrative is action-oriented, depicting threat and resolution, and the outline follows the narrated events with no subpoints for nuance and detail.

Let's start with the immediate context of the account. The narrator begins with the report that the nations in Canaan were used by God to test the Israelites (3:1–6) about matters of war and their obedience to divine commandments. This perspective shapes the way the several stories in the book are presented. A first, quite brief account has the Israelites doing what was evil in the Lord's sight, with the result that the Lord "sold" them into the control of an Aramaean king (3:7–11). The Israelites cry out to the Lord regarding their circumstances and the Lord raised up a deliverer for them named Othniel. He led a successful struggle against the Aramaeans and their king, with the result that the land had rest for forty years. This concise report has a basic pattern of sin, oppression, and deliverance, a motif that a reader of Judges will recognize. That motif is sketched out in 2:11–22.

The story of Ehud begins with the report that "the Israelites *again* did what was evil in the sight of the Lord and the Lord strengthened King Eglon of Moab against Israel." The "again" provides a context for readers. There are also initial details of possible historical importance in 3:13–14. Eglon is a Moabite ruler who worked with the Ammonites and Amalekites to subjugate Israel, and the city of palms was his base of operations. Ammon and Moab were people groups whose traditional territories were east of the Jordan River and the Dead Sea. The Amalekites were a pastoralist tribal society located primarily on the southern and eastern edges of Canaan. According to Genesis 19:30–38, Ammon and Moab were related to Israel through Abraham and his nephew Lot. The Amalekites were fierce opponents (e.g., Exod. 17:8–16). Intriguingly, the city of palms is not otherwise identified in the brief account. Interpreters typically identify it with Jericho. Their reasons for doing so are good examples of historical analysis (cf. Judg. 1:16). Jericho is the best-known city (and one of few) located near Gilgal and the fords of the Jordan River, two entities mentioned in the account; and palm trees are characteristic of it in both ancient and modern times. This, of course, does not mean that Jericho is the city of palms, only that consideration of the historical and geographical setting provided in the account makes it the most plausible identification. Geography is an important consideration in historical analysis. If a Moabite king is living (even part-time) west of the Jordan River, then it is an indication of a successful expansionist policy in gaining the upper hand against Israelite tribal elements. The same thing could be said of the Ammonites (cf. Judg. 10:9).

Let's probe these details a bit more in considering the account. The narrator indicates specifically that it was the *Israelites* who sinned and it was *Israel* that Eglon subjugated. The narrator uses *Israel* as a national term. It is perhaps easy to read more national identity in the term *Israel* than the circumstances of the time warrant. This is a historical judgment and subject to a balance of probability and the weighing of various types of evidence. The narrator writes from a time when monarchy and a more developed national identity had emerged, and thus looks back with that perspective in mind. This is similar to someone writing about colonial America and the struggle against British control, assuming an emerging "national" identity for the colonies in a stage of fruition. Historically, frictions with the British in colonial America varied from colony to colony and even town to town. What happened in Boston, for example, might not affect matters in Charleston in the same way. This analogy would hold for many of the stories of oppression and deliverance in the book of Judges. Regional struggles have taken on a national hue in their retelling. It is historically unlikely, for example, that a Moabite ruler based in Jericho would have subdued the Israelite tribes north of the Ephraimite hill country, a geographic reference cited in 3:27. Ehud was a Benjaminite, from a small tribe sharing a border with the larger tribe of Ephraim. These are the two tribal entities specifically mentioned in the account (3:15, 27), and it makes historical sense that someone from Benjamin would bring tribute to Eglon. Benjamin and Ephraim are also the two tribes whose traditional boundaries intersected near Jericho (Josh. 18:1–28), with Jericho actually reckoned as a Benjaminite city.

The intended audience would certainly recognize the plausible connections in the story between the Israelite tribes of Benjamin and Ephraim and a Moabite ruler in Jericho, as well as the political and theological problems of dealing with Moab. Note that after the initial reference to Ammonites and Amalekites in 3:13, these entities are not mentioned again. Moabite hegemony had expanded westward at the expense (literally, it seems!) of Israelites living nearby. There are, however, a number of things passed over in the account that might assist in a historical reading. One we've noted already; little is said about how those tribes farther from Jericho and Moab may or may not have been involved with Eglon, the subduer of "Israel." We can expand on this observation by saying that nothing is provided about the status of the Israelite tribes east of the Jordan River and the Dead Sea, who lived near and among the traditional territories of the Moabites and Ammonites. Portions of the tribe of Manasseh lived in the Gilead region. Reuben and Gad were south of them in proximity to Ammon and Moab. As readers we might well wonder if the narrator assumed they, too, were paying tribute to Moab and/or Ammon. That is a plausible conclusion; after all, there are other accounts, biblical and extra-biblical, of Israelites in Transjordan who were subjugated periodically to either Ammon or Moab (cf. Judg. 10:6–11:33; 1 Sam. 11:1–4; Moabite Inscription of King Mesha). But we are faced with silence on the matter. This is not to fabricate a historical problem for the story at hand but, rather, to be reminded to pay attention to the brief and selective details actually provided in the account and to think realistically about how they cohere. The details we have relate to a regional struggle, and it is difficult to extrapolate further from them.

We can expand again on the observation about tribal geography and history by putting the story in 3:12–30 in the context of the book of Judges as a whole. The majority of the book is taken up with accounts of men and women who delivered Israel from the hands of oppressors. Most of the stories share the characteristic we've explored—namely, a regional conflict with a local deliverer—but shaped to fit a national storyline. Let's look briefly at some examples.

Deborah was a judge and prophetess who engineered the defeat of King Jabin of Hazor and his commander named Sisera (4:1–24). She musters troops from Naphtali and Zebulun, two Israelite tribes near the city of Hazor, which is located north of the Sea of Galilee. The song of Deborah (5:1–31), which commemorates the victory, lists six participating tribes. Gideon led Israelite fighters against the Midianites and Amalekites, who raided Israelite farmers at harvest time (chaps. 6–8). He was from the tribe of Manasseh and gathered troops from Asher, Zebulun, and Naphtali. These are tribes from the central and northern inheritance of Israel. Jephthah fought against the Ammonites in Gilead, employing the Israelites who lived there on the east side of the Jordan River (10:6–11:33). And Samson, perhaps the best known judge in the book, fought single-handedly against the Philistines (chaps. 13–16). He was from the small tribe of Dan and lived near the larger tribe of Judah and the major Philistine cities (cf. Josh. 13:3).

What about Moab as a historical entity? Interpreters have data about Moab from Egyptian texts of the Late Bronze Age, the Hebrew Bible, several Moabite inscriptions, and Assyrian texts. Something similar can be said for Ammon. Several Moabite rulers are named in these sources, but Eglon is not among them. Almost all of them date to the ninth century BCE and later. Thus it is possible to reconstruct a partial history of Moab from the Late Bronze Age through the Iron Age II, ending with the Babylonian conquest of southern Canaan in the years 605–582 BCE. The account in Judges 3:12–30, however, stands on its own as a textual resource for Israelite–Moabite relations during the period of the Judges.

TRIBUTE AS A CULTURAL PHENOMENON

According to the account, the Israelites sent tribute to Eglon through Ehud. As we shall see, the payment of tribute was a common phenomenon in the ANE. The "tribute" (*minhah*) sent to Eglon is also used in Hebrew for "gifts" or "presents," since the sending and receiving of "gifts" was a primary way for people to navigate social relationships. Gifts were integral to extended family matters like dowries and bride wealth or for social relations in business and political affairs. In a stratified society, rulers can expect *minhah* from constituents (1 Sam. 10:27; 2 Chron. 17:5). They can exchange them to maintain good relations among themselves (2 Kings 20:12). Correspondence between Late Bronze Age rulers in the ANE shows just how lavish these exchanges could be. And rulers can demand it from those they subjugate (2 Kings 17:3). Taxes collected by rulers are a related phenomenon, but are not presents or tribute as such. The tribute brought to Eglon, which is otherwise un-defined, was almost certainly demanded by the king and likely couched in the vocabulary of gifts to honor him and to confirm his hegemony. According to 2 Kings 3:4, King Mesha of Moab used to pay Israel tribute in the amount of one hundred thou-sand lambs and the wool of one hundred thousand rams. This report describes a period in the mid-ninth century BCE during the time of the Omride Dynasty in Israel, when Israel had he-gemony over Moab. In 1868, a European missionary discov-ered a piece of basalt in the Arab village of Dhiban, east of the Dead Sea, that contained a 34-line inscription commissioned by King Mesha of Moab. The inscription refers to Omri and his offspring, and it provides details on the ways in which Moab freed itself from Israelite hegemony.

In the last century, historians have acquired substantial additional data on the matter of tribute in the ANE, such as the Late Bronze Age correspondence just mentioned. In par-ticular, the archeological discoveries of the material culture of the Assyrian Empire have opened new vistas on the subject. This material culture consists of textual and artifactual data and assists modern readers in better understanding a cen-tral phenomenon well known to the intended audience of the book of Judges. As the dominant political force in the ANE for nearly three centuries (9th–7th centuries BCE), the Assyrians demanded tribute from peoples across the Fertile Crescent, Israel and Judah included, and were scrupulous in recording and depicting the collection of it.

Shalmaneser III, for example, was a Neo-Assyrian ruler from 859 to 824 BCE, who engaged in a series of campaigns in the ANE to expand his holdings in the ANE. Choice of "his" is conscious here, since in his surviving annals the campaigns of the army are often described in the first person. Here is a brief excerpt from the Kurkh Monolith, an inscribed monumental stone that offers details of his western campaign in the year 853 BCE: "I departed from the Euphrates. I approached the city of Aleppo. They were afraid to fight. They seized my feet. I received their tribute of silver (and) gold" (COS II, 263).

This inscription has several references to Shalmaneser's collection of booty, looting of cities, and (as in the excerpt just cited) the reception of tribute. In the concluding section, Shalmaneser refers to a coalition of kings who opposed his westward campaigns. Among them is "Ahab, the Israelite." We mentioned him earlier. He is the son of Omri and a major character in the dramatic narratives of 1 Kings 16:29–22:40. Note also in the text cited the reference to the inhabitants of Aleppo "seizing the feet" of Shalmaneser. This indicates a posture of submission—physical prostration to demonstrate loyalty and surrender. Most likely, the scene described refers to the rulers of Aleppo, who would have brought their tribute to Shalmaneser and "seized his feet" as an initial step to honor him and to plead for mercy.

Later in his reign, Shalmaneser commissioned a sculptured obelisk in black alabaster, with texts depicting his rule and carved panels portraying scenes from it. One of the panels depicts a standing Shalmaneser, with a figure on his knees before him whose head is touching the ground. This is essentially the posture of submission just described. The textual inscription—that is, the caption for this panel—reads: "I received the tribute of Jehu [the man] of Bit Humri: silver, gold, a golden bowl, a golden goblet, golden cups, golden buckets, tin, a staff of the king's hand, [and] javelins" (COS II, 270).

Jehu was an Israelite army officer who instituted a coup against the Omride Dynasty and more particularly, Ahab's family and his widow Jezebel (2 Kings 9:1–10:17). According to the biblical narrative, Jenu was not a member of the royal house. Shalmaneser describes him as from the "house of Omri," which apparently was his way of referring to the kingdom of Israel. As we discussed in chapter 5, the use of "house" to describe kingdoms and dynasties was common in the ANE. The scribe who wrote the text probably first encountered Israel as the land ruled by the Omride Dynasty.[3]

In the Judges 3 account, the detail of bringing Eglon tribute is central to the story, not because it was a novel matter or of an item of antiquarian interest but, rather, because it explains realistically how the crafty and brave Ehud gained access to Eglon in order to assassinate him. Rulers receive and demand tribute; it is a staple of their office. And they receive tribute and accompanying supplicants into their presence in order to demonstrate their royal status. The account is silent with regard to the type of tribute or who (besides generic Israelites) provided it. It does contain the detail that the tribute was carried by a group of people (3:18)—something entirely consistent with the ANE tradition of bringing gold and silver vessels physically before the ruler. The narrator artfully expands on Ehud as "hindered with his right hand," which interpreters have traditionally translated as "left-handed." This may well be correct. Some think that it means Ehud was ambidextrous (following the Greek translation of 3:15) and thus trained to use weapons with either hand. In any case, the facility with the left hand seems to have been a characteristic of Benjaminites (cf. Judg. 20:16). The size and placement of the sword on the (inside) right thigh, where it could be accessed by a left hand, are pertinent details. Apparently it is assumed that a visitor to Eglon would be searched for weapons and that the typical hiding place on the left thigh would be scrutinized. Ehud's craftiness is also illustrated by the manner in which he gained a second, private audience with Eglon. After presenting the tribute to Eglon and departing his presence, he quickly turns around and offers to provide Eglon a "secret message," subsequently qualified as a "message from God" (3:19–20). After receiving the Israelite tribute, the intended audience could well imagine that Eglon assuming a further "gift" of some kind!

MURDER IN A PRIVATE CHAMBER

The murder scene offers several fascinating details and raises intriguing questions. A number of interpreters have intuited humor in the name of the Moabite king and in the manner of his death. *Eglon* means "calf" or "young bull." While it is not unusual for a person to bear an animal name, the description of his stabbing, where the fat encompasses the knife (3:22), suggests that the king was obese. Does this make him a "fat cow" or is that a modern metaphor? The king's servants do not disturb Eglon in his private chamber for a time after the departure of Ehud. The door is locked and they suppose that he may be relieving himself—that is, defecating (3:24). In recent years this comment has caused discussion among some interpreters, who point to the occasional archeological discovery of indoor toilets in structures belonging to upper-class people in the ANE. These range from carved stone seats to channels that use water to carry away waste. Does this mean, for example, that the seat upon which Eglon sat in his upper chamber was a toilet and that Ehud stabbed him while he was relieving himself? On the one hand, historians are right to point to archeological data that potentially illumine the historical context of a story or the time of the narrator who provides it. On the other hand, it is possible to over-interpret details and draw unwarranted conclusions from them. Perhaps Eglon had what has been known for centuries as a "chamber pot" in which to eliminate his waste and the fact that a few structures in antiquity had forms of toilets in them has nothing to do with the detail of Eglon's 'bathroom break," to use a modern term for the servants' supposition about his absence.

READING JUDGES 3:12–30 HISTORICALLY

Reading this account historically can mean several things. For one, it means reading it realistically as an account in Israelite tribal life before the rise of monarchy in early Iron Age Canaan. In this instance, it is plausible that a Moabite king expanded his area of rule to include territory west of the Jordan River and that the tribes of Benjamin and Ephraim paid him tribute. Struggles and negotiated relationships with the Moabites were part of the ebb and flow of life in southern Canaan. This is part of the world behind the text and known to the intended audience. The details, however, are not currently historically verifiable and thus some or all may not be factual. Assessing those matters starts with a close reading of the text and then the weighing of probabilities. Reading the account historically also means considering the setting of the narrator, who writes at some distance from the period described, as well as the narrator's intended audience. Narrator and audience were jointly heirs of several centuries of interaction between the various polities in the region, and they knew full well what tribute and oppression looked like. The book of Judges offers a repetitive cycle of stories detailing the ways in which the Lord handed over a disobedient Israel to oppressors and then raised up deliverers for them. This motif is the major shaping element in the book's explanatory presentations of pre-monarchic history.

"There was no king in Israel" (Judg. 21:25). The book of Judges concludes with the report that "there was no king in Israel and people did what was right in their own eyes." According to the narrator of 1 Samuel, at a subsequent point during the period of Judges, the Israelites sought a king so that he could "govern (*shaphat*) us and go before us and fight our battles" (8:20). Like the book of Ruth, 1 Samuel continues with a portrait of the period of the Judges as the national storyline transitions to monarchy. Kingship, like any form of governance, had its positive and negative attributes, and Samuel's response to the people's request lists some of the negatives (8:11–17). So centuries of regional difficulties and the rise of monarchy are in the background of the historical narrative in Judges 3:12–30. The narrator and the intended audience look back at it to see the hand of the Lord at work in a national storyline, an unfolding narrative of which they are a part.

8

Narrative Contexts

History and Culture, Continued

IN THE PREVIOUS CHAPTER WE introduced *Downton Abbey*, a historical period television series, as a modern example of a story that explains the past as it entertains viewers. A second illustration comes in the ten-hour historical documentary, *O J Simpson: Made in America*, produced by the ESPN television network and shown to critical acclaim in June 2016. It chronicled the life of Orenthal James Simpson, a star college and professional football player, a sports commentator and actor, who was arrested in 1994 for the murder of his estranged wife and her acquaintance in Brentwood, California. The criminal trial went on for months, was televised live, and proved to be a public sensation. Mr. Simpson was found not guilty. He was subsequently convicted in a civil judgment related to their deaths, which required no jail time, and later still was tried and convicted of robbery in Las Vegas, Nevada. Mr. Simpson is an African American; his wife and her acquaintance were Caucasians, adding matters of race and culture to a compelling murder mystery and its aftermath.

As with *Downton Abbey*, the documentary is a superb historical period drama, this time dealing with historical persons in the context of the sports and entertainment worlds of the late twentieth century. And it, too, offers multiple analogies and insights into the ways of portraying the past in HB narratives. Like many biblical narratives, it has a lot of dialogue. The producers extensively interviewed dozens of people and used excerpts from them to present perspectives on the events in question. The documentary also used detailed footage from testimonies in the criminal trial. It is possible, for example, to come away from viewing the documentary with more questions than answers about the murders themselves, but the dialogues offer multiple windows into the people and events chronicled in it.

The documentary patiently shows how people weigh evidence (including contradictory data) and seek to reconstruct a plausible narrative from it. When all was said and done at the trial, there were gaps in both evidence and the coherence of the competing narratives created by the opposing legal teams. Gaps in data and fragmentary sources are even more frequent for ancient narratives, given the passage of time. And there are no survivors from antiquity to interview! The criminal trial of Mr. Simpson became center stage for the difficult cultural conversation in America over historic racial disparities, the treatment of celebrities, and difficulties in the justice system. As the documentary makes clear, the majority of African Americans believed that Mr. Simpson was innocent of the double murder, while the majority of Caucasian Americans, looking at the same evidence, believed he was guilty. The point here is not who is correct but, rather, that the perception of truth and meaning in any one situation is shaped by larger cultural forces. African Americans repeatedly noted how police have rushed to judgment when the suspect is a black man, and many discounted the motives and methods of the police investigation. Many white Americans saw a rich celebrity defended by a "dream team" of lawyers getting away with murder.

The documentary well illustrates the paradigm we've noted previously about the different worlds of a narrative. There is the world of the text itself, which readers engage and assess.

There is the world behind the text—what we think of as the historical and cultural contexts—from which the text emerges. In the case of Mr. Simpson, there are the details of his life set in the larger matrix of late twentieth-century life in the United States. And there is the world in front of the text. This is the context of the reader, whose own life experience shapes the way a narrative about the past can be engaged. In the summer of 2016, American society was roiled by several police shootings of African American men, with the result that a protest movement developed using the name "Black Lives Matter." This context provided a lens through which to look back in time at a previous national conversation about crime and racial tensions and to see to what extent the passing of a couple decades allowed for a different perspective on what some called the "trial of the century."

THE CULTURAL CONTEXTS OF MARRIAGE IN THE BOOK OF RUTH

We've looked already at the short story of Ruth from several angles. The marriage between Ruth and Boaz is integral to the plot of the book, and the commitments made by Ruth and Boaz are central to the rendering of their characters. We've already noted aspects of the tribal custom of a male relative taking a widow in marriage to produce an heir for a deceased husband. That goal—the production of an heir for the deceased—is explicitly cited in the negotiation between Boaz and Mr. So-and-so (Ruth 4:5, 10). And we indicated briefly that some interpreters conclude that the book of Ruth emerged as a counter to more exclusive ways of understanding marriage in Israel. We want to look further at some cultural aspects of Boaz and Ruth's marriage as an exercise in historical reading. In turn, this will take us to other narratives in the HB for additional perspective on that task.

Let's return to a previously asked question: What difference does it make that Ruth is Moabite? One plausible response is that it doesn't make any difference in the narrative, at least regarding her marrying either Mr. So-and-so or Boaz. While she is "Ruth the Moabite," the wife of Mahlon (4:5, 10), the matter at hand in the gate transaction seems to be her status as a widow of child-bearing age, who had married into the clan of Elimelech. She is thus connected to the clan property nominally held by her mother-in-law Naomi on behalf of deceased male relatives, including her husband Mahlon. Her Moabite identity is possibly incidental. On the other hand, her ethnicity is a characteristic that stands out in the account. The narrator, for example, indicates repeatedly that Ruth is a Moabite (1:22; 2:2, 6, 21); she describes herself as a foreigner in the initial encounter with Boaz (2:10); and Boaz acknowledges that she had left her homeland in coming to Bethlehem, where she now dwells under the protection of the Lord, the God of Israel (2:11–12). Because of these data one could also answer plausibly that her ethnicity is central to her character and to the significance of the plot for the intended audience. How might that intended audience react to her ethnicity? This last matter is an important element in a historical reading of the text, where probing of the world behind the text may reveal a cultural matrix that influenced the telling of the story and its reception by both intended and later readers.

Let's ask a further question: Are there other Israelites who married Moabite women and what do we know about those relationships? King Solomon reportedly married many foreign women (1 Kings 11:1–13), including at least one from Moab. The narrator of 1 Kings reports these marriages—700 princesses and 300 concubines—and cites instruction that the Lord gave the Israelites regarding the nations of Canaan when they entered the Promised Land: "you shall not enter into marriages with them, nor shall they with you; for they will certainly entice you to follow their gods" (11:2). This is not a formal quote from another biblical text, but it is a paraphrase of the instructions contained in Deuteronomy 7:3 and there are similar thoughts/warnings expressed elsewhere (Exod. 34:16; Josh. 23:12–13; Judg. 3:5–6). In Solomon's case, he also built a shrine on the hill east of the Jerusalem temple for his Moabite spouse(s) and others, who wished to worship Chemosh, the chief Moabite deity. The narrator reports that this made the Lord angry with Solomon and it contributed to the breakup of the tribal nation of Israel (1 Kings 11:9–40). As we shall see (Neh. 13:26), others cite Solomon's marriages as a negative example for Israel.

Interpreters ancient and modern also recognize that Solomon's many marriages were the result of diplomatic and economic ties in the region. A king in his day would use marriage to solidify regional ties, whether he himself married a foreign princess or arranged marriages for his sons and daughters with prominent families. Nevertheless, the compilers of 1 Kings see Solomon's marriage with foreign women as a detriment to the spiritual health of Israel.

The book of Numbers preserves intertwined stories about the negative effects of foreign women on the spiritual and moral health of Israel (Num. 25:1–18). As the Israelites prepared to enter the land of Canaan from east of the Jordan River, they camped at a place called Shittim. It is in a region on the east side of the Jordan River, across from Jericho, known as the Plains of Moab (22:1; cf. 33:49). According to the narrative, Israelite men had sexual relations with Moabite women and the people were drawn into the worship of Moabite deities, provoking an angry response from the Lord (25:1–5). One of those deities was known as the Baal (Lord or Master) of Peor. The prophet Hosea later recalled this engagement with Baal of Peor as a negative example for his audience (9:10). The Midianites and one of their women are also part of the debacle in the Plains of Moab (25:6–18).

One can see from these examples that various writers in the HB regarded marriage with foreign women to be a detriment to the spiritual and moral health of Israel. We noted in chapter 3 that compilers of the books of Ezra and Nehemiah saw the marriages between Jewish men and foreign women to be a crisis for Jewish existence in the Persian period. In what follows, we will look at some texts from these two books that deals with this subject, and we will use the data to explore further the practice of reading HB narratives historically.

MARRIAGE IN JERUSALEM ACCORDING TO THE BOOKS OF EZRA AND NEHEMIAH

According to the books of Ezra and Nehemiah, some groups of Jews in the diaspora (i.e., the dispersion of Israelites and Judahites by the Assyrians and Babylonians) returned to Jerusalem and the Persian province of Yehud to further develop Jewish life in its ancestral setting. *Yehud* is the Aramaic term for Judah. *Jews* is a derivative term from Judahites and a word that came to describe people descended from tribal Israel, whether they were from Judah/Yehud or another tribe. The rule of the Persian Empire and the return of some Jews to their homeland during it begin what interpreters call the post-exilic period.

The events described in the book of Ezra are not given in chronological order, but they cover several decades of time. The first half of the book is a summary, beginning with the notice that King Cyrus of Persia allowed Jews who worshiped the God of Heaven, also known as the Lord, the God of Israel, to return and rebuild the temple in Jerusalem (Ezra 1:1–4; 539/38 BCE).

This sets the stage for Ezra's subsequent travel to Jerusalem. His work in Jerusalem is described in the last three chapters in the book (8–10). There were difficulties to overcome and opposition among inhabitants of the region to the return of Jewish immigrants. These difficulties included cultural, economic, and religious tensions. The book of Nehemiah offers even more details on these difficulties. One point of tension and anguish was marriage between Jewish men and non-Jewish women. Both the work of Ezra and that of Nehemiah are set in the reign of the Persian king Artaxerxes. More than one Persian ruler bore this name. Scholars debate which monarch is in view in the two books, particularly for Ezra. Here are some relevant dates:

Cyrus ruled over a united Persian Empire 539–530 BCE
Artaxerxes ruled 465–424 BCE
Artaxerxes II ruled 404–358

For our purposes, we need not work through the options and make a firm decision on dating the work of either Ezra or Nehemiah, while we keep before us the historical-cultural context of the post-exilic period and life in the Persian province of Yehud. Ezra, a Jewish scribe and priest from Babylon, came to Jerusalem in the seventh year of Artaxerxes, which would be either 458 or 398 BCE. Nehemiah, a Jewish official from Susa, came as governor of Yehud in Artaxerxes's twentieth year (Neh. 2:5). After twelve years of work, he returned to Susa, only to come back later to Jerusalem (Neh. 13:6–7). Likely his first trip to Jerusalem was in the year 445.

Ezra

As indicated, in reading Ezra one encounters several religious and cultural tensions between the Jews who returned to Yehud and those inhabitants, Jewish or otherwise, who lived there or in nearby territory. Literarily speaking, tensions over marriage and Jewish identity dominate the presentation of Ezra's work in Jerusalem (Ezra 8:31–10:44). As a priest and scribe, Ezra was "skilled in the law of Moses," and he came from Babylon to Jerusalem with the support of the Persian king to assist the community in the reconstruction of Jewish life and worship (7:1–26). After a summary of gifts for the temple and an impressive worship service (8:31–36), the narrator concludes the book with an account of the community's responses to the crisis of mixed marriages.

Ezra 9–10 can be outlined as follows:

    I. Officials inform Ezra of the problem of mixes marriages   9:1–4
   II. Ezra fasts and confesses community guilt   9:5–15
  III. Ezra and people gather in temple courtyard   10:1–6
      A. Ezra continues fasting and praying   10:1
      B. Shecaniah urges divorce of foreign wives   10:2–4
      C. Ezra urges compliance and people concur   10:5
      D. Ezra prays overnight in temple chamber   10:6
   IV. Proclamation for gathering of former exiles   10:7–8
    V. Assembly of former exiles in Jerusalem   10:9–15
      A. Ezra urges confession and divorce of foreign wives   10:10–11
      B. Assembly agrees on a process for divorce   10:12–14
      C. Some opposed to policy   10:15
   VI. Commission identifies men married to foreigners   10:16–23
  VII. Summary statement on divorce proceedings   10:44

The outline briefly presents a series of actions, prayer, and communal dialogue. Ezra responds on more than one occasion to reports from contemporaries, and people respond to him by way of oath and swearing (9:1; 10:2–5, 12). His actions take place in the temple precincts. There he fasts, mourns, tears his garments, and prays, whether in the courtyard after the evening sacrifice or in the chamber of a priest named Jehohanan. The majority of chapter 9 is prayer of confession. While it is presented as Ezra's prayer, it contains several first-person plural pronouns. He thus represents Israel through his confession of guilt, which also contains a résumé of God's dealings with the people and their current status. Those who have returned to Jerusalem from the diaspora are a "remnant." Although Persian subjects, God has granted them "new life" to set up the temple (9:8–9). Their guilt consists in rejecting the words of "prophets," who warned that the inhabitants of Canaan made the land "polluted" and "unclean," and who instructed Israel not to intermarry with them (9:10–12).

We should note some other terms from the prayer and its context. The first is the "holy seed" (9:2, a phrase used to characterize the "remnant"; 9:8, 13) of former Israel and Judah now living in Yehud. The officials who come to Ezra use it to describe the returned exiles, who have "mixed themselves" with the peoples of the land. Thus the two parts of chapter 9 reinforce one another: the officials describe for Ezra a faithless activity (9:1–4), which he, in turn, confesses before God as corporate guilt and the cause of judgment upon the people. The narratives in Ezra also use the terms "separate/separation" (*badal*) to characterizes the religious practices and community of Judaism in distinction from the peoples of the land and their pollution (6:21, 9:1, 10:11). Separation from the peoples of the land is the preferred action rather than "mixing" with them.

In chapter 10, a representative of the people addresses Ezra and urges that they (the people) make a covenant to "send away all these wives and their children . . . and let it be done according to the law" (v. 3). An assembly of people subsequently takes place in Jerusalem. Ezra then sets up a council to examine matters and to identify men with foreign wives. A list of them is produced. They are to "separate themselves [*badal*] from the peoples of the land and their foreign wives" (10:11). Interestingly, there is brief mention of opposition to the proposal of divorcing foreign wives, but no context or reason is provided for it (10:15).

Nehemiah

The narratives in the book of Nehemiah have similarities with those in Ezra. Both use first-person reports—what interpreters sometimes call memoirs—and they bristle with issues of community tensions. A corporate confession of sin is central to both, as are the responses of the people in oath and ceremony to bind themselves to the instructions of Torah as the basis of institutional life (Neh. 9–10). While the issue of mixed marriages dominates the description of Ezra's time in Jerusalem, it is but one of several problems that engaged Nehemiah.

In Nehemiah 9:2, those who assemble for a fast and confession are described as having "separated themselves [*badal*] from all foreigners." This is terminology and practice like that in Ezra. Perhaps we have identified a theme for the book. Nehemiah also stresses the importance of reading from the Torah (8:1–18, 13:1–3). Behind this emphasis is likely the work of Ezra and others in formulating the written Torah as the basis for Jewish life and identity. Knowledge of Mosaic tradition and priestly lore was Ezra's specialty (Ezra 7:6, 10). The Torah, what we also call the Pentateuch, likely reached its final form in the post-exilic period, and Ezra may well have had a hand in this important endeavor. In any case, Ezra and Nehemiah represent the concerns succinctly expressed in Leviticus 20:26 for the Israelite community: "You shall be holy to me because I the Lord am holy, and I have separated [*badal*] you from other peoples to be mine."

According to Nehemiah 13:1–3, the book of Moses was read to the people. When they heard that no "Ammonite or Moabite should enter the "assembly of God," the people "separated [*badal*] from Israel those of foreign descent." The ban on Ammonites and Moabites is given in Deuteronomy 23:3–5, a passage we have previously noted. The syntax of Nehemiah 13:3 indicates that Jews who followed the reforms of Nehemiah and Ezra removed foreigners or those of mixed descent from among themselves. This is a complementary move with that described in Nehemiah 9:2, whereby those of Israelite descent separated themselves from those of foreign identity.

Nehemiah reports briefly that he saw Jewish men who had married women from Ashdod (Philistine and Canaanite descent), Ammon, and Moab (13:23–27). He physically abused the men and made them swear an oath not to allow their sons or daughters to marry such persons. In arguing against intermarriage, the case of Solomon is cited as a negative example (13:26). In a related matter, Nehemiah chased away the grandson of the high priest, who had married the daughter of Sanballat the Horonite (13:28–29). Sanballat was from Samaria, an official of the Persian Empire and someone who opposed Nehemiah on several occasions (e.g., 6:1–14). Neither his political actions nor his form of Judaism was acceptable to Nehemiah.

DEFINING ISRAELITE IDENTITY IN THE POST-EXILIC PERIOD

The concerns to define faithful Yahwism are rooted in the cultural and historical context of exile and return. Perhaps we might think of the figures of Ezra and Nehemiah as architects of a Jewish identity that emerged from the trauma of exile and the crises presented by the options of assimilation and syncretism. They were not alone in their concerns to define a faithful people in the Persian Empire. The short story of Esther recounts a pogrom proposed against Jews in the empire and the ways that the pogrom was averted by the efforts of a Jew named Mordecai and his cousin Esther. She had become queen, but had not revealed her heritage to the king. It is a drama filled with irony and reversals and vindication of the Jews against their Persian opponents led by an official named Haman. Haman tells the Persian king Ahasuerus (Greek Xerxes) that Jews are a people whose customary laws are different from other peoples in his vast realm, that they do not follow Persian laws, and that it was not in his best interests to tolerate them (3:8). The narrative is less about intra-Jewish debates of self-definition and more about a chilling and irrational response to Judaism.

Something related is portrayed in the narratives of Daniel 1–6 and their presentation of Jewish exiles in Babylon. Daniel and his three friends do not eat the food provided for them at the Babylonian court (1:3–16). This shows the concern of Jews to maintain a dietary code and not become defiled by pagan food. The four Hebrew exiles do not engage in pagan and polytheistic religious practices, either, a profile for which they were persecuted. In recognition of Jerusalem's sanctity, Daniel opens his windows toward that city and prays three times a day (6:10). These narratives represent the distinctiveness of Jewish practices and the persecution that may come upon Jews as a result.

A prayer of confession later in the book (Dan. 9:4–19) has similarities with the confessional prayers in Nehemiah 9 and Ezra 9. All three portray the exile of Israel as judgment for transgressing God's laws. In Daniel and Esther, the righteousness of Torah practices and Jewish distinctiveness can result in oppressive responses from others. Ezra and Nehemiah reflect some of that as well, related primarily to the suspicion and hostility the returning exiles incurred from the local population. One difference is that Ezra and Nehemiah are working in the province of Yehud, while Daniel and Esther depict Jews as a persecuted minority in the diaspora. All these books, however, assume that the exile brought about pressures on Israelite identity, whether that pressure was generated externally from pagans or internally among Jews.

The reform efforts of Ezra and Nehemiah thus reveal certain divisions within the larger Jewish community of Yehud over the degree of separation from the peoples of the land, including tensions with forms of Judaism represented by people like Sanballat. There is additional evidence for this debate over separation elsewhere in post-exilic texts. The prophetic oracle in Isaiah 56:1–8, for example, represents foreigners "joined" to the Lord as saying that the Lord should not "separate [*badal*] them from his people," and the Lord declaring that the temple in Jerusalem shall be a "house of prayer" for all people. The verb "separate" is the same one used repeatedly in Ezra and Nehemiah.

We should not assume, of course, that concern for self-identification and distinctive religious practices were limited to Jews in the post-exilic period. In some form or another, these concerns were part of Israelite identity as far back as the HB can take its readers. Consider again, for example, the narratives in the book of Genesis concerned with the origins of Israel's ancestors (Gen. 12–50). They have roots in the pre-monarchic period, even as they are shaped centuries later for inclusion in the Torah. Abraham, for example, instructs his servant to go to Abraham's kin to secure a wife for Isaac, since he did not want Isaac to marry a woman from the Canaanites, among whom Abraham lived (Gen. 24:2–4). While this may reflect a desire of separation from or antipathy toward Canaanites, it also reflects a common practice among Semitic peoples—namely, endogamous marriage, or the custom of marrying within the larger clan or tribe. Jacob follows this custom in marrying Rachel and Leah (29–30). When Esau married Hittite women (26:34–35), it was a source of frustration to his mother (27:46). He later married a daughter of Ishmael, who was part of the Abrahamic family (28:6–8), even though neither the Edomites nor the Ishmaelites always got along with the line of Isaac and Jacob. Judah married Shua, a Canaanite woman (38:2) and Joseph married Asenath, the daughter of an Egyptian priest (41:45). Given the custom of endogamous marriage and the desire to maintain a distinctive identity among the Canaanite peoples, neither marriage is described as an impropriety.

Thus, on the one hand, there are narratives in the HB and instructions in the Torah that represent the importance of distinctive practices of the Israelite faith and the need for separation from the pagan peoples of the land. On the other hand, there are narratives and other texts that recognize the significance of interaction with non-Israelites and the contributions of foreigners to Israelite faith and practice.

RUTH THE MOABITE AND THE WORLD BEHIND HER STORY

We can circle back to the earlier question regarding the story of Ruth the Moabite, who marries into the tribe of Judah and the clan of Perez. A plausible case can be made that the book was written in the post-exilic period and that the narrator wanted to address the simmering issue of separation from foreigners. After all, not only is Ruth a foreigner but also she is a Moabite, one of the peoples singled out elsewhere in the HB as dangerous to the spiritual health of Israel and Judah. This might be one reason that the narrator indicates repeatedly that Ruth is a Moabite. She thus makes a good case to engage the rigorous practices of separation inculcated in Ezra and Nehemiah, including the opposition to mixed marriages, with the claim that ethnicity is less important than commitments and character. She who came to dwell under the wings of the Lord (Ruth 2:12), and who showed unwavering commitment to the family in which she married, is no threat to the house of Israel. Like Rachel, Leah, and Tamar (probably a Canaanite), Ruth helped to build it.

Discerning the time and circumstances of the book's origin is a key component in the historical analysis of a biblical book. A decision that Ruth is a post-exilic work depends on the analysis of its Hebrew text and the contents of the narrative. To then read the book as a counterpoint to the separatist reforms of Ezra and Nehemiah is a second decision in historical analysis. It assumes, again plausibly, that simmering issues at the reconstructed time of writing (i.e., the world behind the text) are addressed by the narrator through the medium of telling a story about a different time and place in the history of Israel.

A plausible case can also be made that the Hebrew text and the contents of the narrative are pre-exilic in origin (perhaps 8th/7th centuries BCE), even if the account is later supplemented by the genealogy in 4:18–22. Drawing on traditions about the tribe of Judah and the ancestors of King David, the narrator shows how God's work with the ancestors continued into the period of the Judges, with the surprising marriage of an Ephrathite to a Moabite woman. In terms of historical analysis, the story would favorably explicate a stubborn tradition (plausibly factual), that King David had a Moabite ancestress, a tradition that would not otherwise reflect favorably on him. Her strength of character and her ready acceptance of the Israelite ethos made her a vessel of God's providential work, just as David was later a chosen vessel to lead the people of Israel.

Which literary and historical analysis is correct? Or does another reconstruction seem more likely? Both options have the support of competent scholars, and it is a fascinating exercise to sort through the data in forming a conclusion. One should weigh the data carefully and recognize the influence of controlling assumptions in coming to a conclusion. For example, does the narrative of Ruth impress you as a polemical account or one designed to counter an opposing narrative? And if so, what story or idea does it intend to counter? Let's go back to the introductory portion of the chapter. The documentary on the life and times of OJ Simpson showed how societal and cultural identities influenced the way that people sorted out his "story" and responded to it. Correspondingly, cultural factors were at work whenever the book of Ruth was written (the world behind the text). We want to explore that background for whatever contributions it can make to our understanding, even as we recognize the hypothetical nature of reading the narrative in light of a reconstructed historical matrix. As later readers, we are not the intended audience of the book. In a sense, we look over their shoulders in responding to it.

And there is another factor to consider from the introductory example. The documentary on Simpson's life was shown twenty-plus years after the sensational murders at the heart of the presentation. As briefly noted, those who watched the documentary in 2016 did so in the context of a series of shootings of black men that roiled American society and exposed passions and suspicions from various points of view. We can describe that as the world in front of the documentary, a nexus of experience and commitments that influenced the way to interpret a presentation about the past. If, for example, the book of Ruth was not written in the post-exilic period to make a point about the viability of God's people mixing with and marrying foreigners, concerns about such marriages were part of the world in front of the text for post-exilic hearers/ readers. Moreover, the fact that the books of Ruth, Ezra, and Nehemiah were all included in Israel's canonical texts means that generations of readers have had to put them in dialogue with each other!

Contemporary readers of these three narratives may have vastly different assumptions about marriage and ethnic interchange from those of ancient writers. It is in recognizing the influence of the world in front of the text—a world that can both constrict and expand response—that readers can be more engaged with a classic narrative from the past and the historical circumstances proposed for it.

Section III

THE WORLDS OF

AND BEHIND THE TEXT

9

Genesis 2

Marriage and Family

WE HAVE LOOKED AT MORE than one narrative where marriage and family play a role. In this chapter we will look at Genesis 2:4–25, a brief narrative where these matters are also in view. It is part of the etiological portrait of primeval time in Genesis 1–3. One of the best-known stories in the HB, this account has captured the imagination of readers over the centuries with its depiction of a garden planted by the Lord God and the creation of a man and woman to live and work in it. There are many avenues of interest that we might pursue, but our focus is on the literary and thematic portraits of man and woman's origins.

OUTLINE AND OVERVIEW

Here is an outline of the passage.
  I. The earth becomes a habitable place   2:4–7
     A. No rain or plants, but ground water   2:4–6
     B. The Lord God forms a man, a living being   2:7
  II. The Garden of Eden as the first home for human beings   2:8–23
     A. The Lord God plants a garden in Eden   2:8a
     B. The Lord God places the man in the garden   2:8b

The passage begins with a brief description of the earth as a habitable setting, but one needing some changes before it would be suitable for human beings. It is not clear where the passage begins. Some interpreters understand 2:4a to be a concluding comment for an initial account of creation that began with Genesis 1:1. If correct, our passage would begin with 2:4b and the temporal clause, "in the day that the Lord God made the earth and the heavens. . . ." We'll have more to say about the immediate context for our passage, but let's begin with the proposal that 2:4a is a heading, an introductory statement that receives elaboration in what follows. The reason to think of 2:4a as an introductory statement is that its phrase "these are the generations [*toledot*]" is used similarly nine other times in the book of Genesis, where it introduces a genealogy or points to stories that follow about members of a family line (6:9; 10:1; 11:10, 27; 25:12, 19; 36:1, 9; 37:2).[1] Admittedly the earth and heavens don't have a genealogy or produce generations the way human beings do. The Hebrew word *toledot* in 2:4 has the sense of a record or account. A similar introductory phrase in Genesis 5:1 uses the Hebrew word *toledot* and is followed by a temporal clause describing God's prior activity: "This is the record of the generations [*toledot*]" of Adam. In the day God created man (i.e., humankind), God created him in the image of God."

How, therefore, did the world of earth and heaven, with its plants, animals, and human beings, originate? In brief, that is what 2:4a introduces and what Genesis 2:4b–25 provides.

The Lord God formed a man from the dust of the ground and breathed into his nostrils so that he became a "living being." We might call him "the earth creature," since the Hebrew text plays on the connection between the 'adam, a term that can refer to a single man or collectively to the human race (cf. Gen. 1:26), and the word "earth" ('adamah), the material used to form the man. Then the Lord God planted a garden in Eden, placed the man in it, and brought forth plants from the ground. Note the comment in 2:9 that two named trees are in the garden. One is the tree of life and the other is the tree of the knowledge of good and evil, which were in the midst of the garden! Both will play a significant role for human life in Eden.

ELABORATING ON EDEN AND ITS INHABITANTS (GENESIS 2:7–25)

Eden has headwaters that nourish the garden and feed four rivers (2:10–14) that flow from it and that water the earth. The description of these phenomena follows a common Hebrew narrative style. The making of the garden is first indicated and then some aspect of it receives elaboration. Something similar is done with the notice that God formed the man and placed him in the garden (2:7–8); his place there will receive elaboration in 2:15–25. Indeed, this literary style results in the narrative twice indicating that God had placed the man in the garden (2:8, 15). Something similar, furthermore, may be at work when 2:2–25 is read as an elaboration on an initial account of origins given in Genesis 1:1–2:3.

The name *Eden* itself indicates fullness or abundance. Readers will recognize two of the river names, Tigris and

Euphrates. The other two names, Pishon and Gihon, are obscure, and it is an interesting question whether the other names were recognized by earlier readers and associated with known bodies of water or whether they derive from primitive traditions and contributed to a sense that Eden is no longer a place that can be reached. Note, for example, the way the prophet Ezekiel employs the traditions of Eden as God's garden over against the pretensions of the king of Tyre and Egypt's pharaoh, both of whom will be judged and found wanting (Ezek. 28:11–19, 31:1–18). The Tyrian king is depicted as having been expelled from Eden, while the Assyrian Empire, which had beauty like that of Eden and then collapsed, is a warning to the pharaoh about judgment to come.

The man is tasked with work in the garden. Eden's fruitfulness will be of benefit to him, but there is also an explicit limit on his place there. He is not to eat of the tree of the knowledge of good and evil, as he may of every other tree, with death as the penalty for disobedience. This prohibition and consequence is conveyed directly to the man in speech from the Lord God.

According to the Lord God, it is not good for the man to be alone. More specifically, the man needs a "helper as a partner" (NRSV), someone who corresponds to him. None of the animals, however, was suitable for the man. The same Hebrew phrase, meaning essentially "corresponding to" or "suitable for him" occurs in verses 18 and 20. The man interacts with the Lord God, who made him and the garden, and with the animals he names, but neither deity nor animals is the suitable companion corresponding to him.

The Lord God, then, brings a deep sleep upon the man, removes a side bone (traditionally understood to be a rib) from him, and proceeds to make a woman. Upon seeing her, the man exclaims (2:23): "Now this one is bone of my bone and flesh of my flesh. This one shall be called woman [ishah] because this one was taken from man [ish]." The English rendering shows something of the poetic wordplay in the original, where the demonstrative pronoun (*z'ot*; "this one") is used three times for emphasis. The intimate, suitable correspondence between man and woman is confirmed by the etymological connection of the words (*ish* and *ishah*) and the sharing of bone and flesh.

What else might this correspondence mean? When a man leaves his father and mother—and human parents have not been mentioned previously in Genesis 2!—he is joined to his wife (*ishah*) and they become "one flesh" (2:24). We will look later at this phrase, but in context it also represents the sought-for correspondence. The narrator then indicates that the man and woman were naked, but not ashamed (2:25). This comment brings the passage to a conclusion and prepares the reader for further developments in the Eden narrative.

TAKING NOTE OF SOME VOCABULARY

We noted that the Hebrew word *toledot*, typically translated as "generation," is used multiple times in the book of Genesis. In chapter 2, we discussed briefly that the repeated use of this term reflects a structuring device for the book's narrative, organizing the contents as a connected story, and emphasizing the kinship connections of Israel's ancestors, whom God chose as vessels of blessing to the families and nations of the earth. Our passage introduces the first couple, whose descendants will populate the earth and from whom come the ancestors of Israel.

The deity is referred to as the "Lord God" eleven times in the account. "Lord" is the English rendering of the personal name of God, often pronounced as Yah-weh (cf. Exod. 3:1–15). This compound name is not used in Genesis 1:1–2:3, where "God" (*'elohim*) is used exclusively. In the continuation of the Eden narrative in Genesis 3, the name "Lord God" is used nine times, but only four times in the rest of Genesis. Interpreters have used these data (and others) to support the conclusion that the account of creation in Genesis 1:1–2:3 originates from a different source or sources from that in 2:4–25. Correspondingly, these data (and others) support the conclusion that 3:1–24 derives from the same source(s) as 2:4–25.

We have referred repeatedly to "the man" (*ha'adam*) in 2:4–25. The noun *'adam* occurs sixteen times and all but once with the definite article (*ha*; "the"). We even referred to him as "the earth creature," given his origins in the dust of the ground (*'adamah*). The one exception is verse 20, where the Hebrew text has "but for Adam, no helper was found that corresponded to him." Without the definite article, we would naturally take the noun as a proper name (Adam), which is the way it is rendered in some modern translations of the verse. A similar phenomenon occurs in the continuation of the Eden story in Genesis 3. There, too, the account has "the man" (3:8, 9, 12, 20, 22, 24; cf. 4:1), but twice it is *'adam* (3:17, 21). Some translations render the noun consistently as "the man" throughout Genesis 2–3 (cf. NRSV), while others may render one or more of those lacking the definite article as the personal name "Adam," a usage that is confirmed in Genesis 4:25 and 5:1 (cf. 1 Chron. 1:1). These data are another reason to consider Genesis 3 as a continuation of the source(s) in Genesis 2:4–25.

The Lord God formed the man from the ground and breathed the breath of life into his nostrils. This made him a "living being" (2:8), like the "living beings," the animals that God also made from the ground. While the man and the animals are similar in origin, there are differences as well. The man is to tend and keep the garden. And the man names the animals, reflecting another form of hierarchy. He has the power of speech, both to name other creatures (2:19) and to converse with God. And as noted, he is also *'ish*, a word that has the semantic range of "man" and "husband" in the Eden narrative.

The word *'ishah* is used similarly in Genesis 2. It is rendered "woman" in the play on the word *'ish* in 2:23 and as "wife" in 2:24. In 3:20, the woman/wife is given the name Eve, a play on the word for life/living (*hay*). As her husband puts it, she is the "mother of all living [human beings]." These connections between man and woman bring us back to the Lord God's declaration in 2:18 that the man needs a "helper" (*'ezer*) who adequately corresponds to him, a role that none of the animals could fulfill (2:20). The noun "helper" is used overwhelmingly in the HB to refer to divine assistance. In 2:18 and 20, the term "helper" apparently refers analogously to abilities possessed by the woman that neither the man nor the animals had.

Man and woman share "bone and flesh," and together become "one flesh." These phrases have kinship connotations (Gen. 29:14; Judg. 9:2; 2 Sam. 19:12–13). The term "flesh" by itself can be used similarly (Gen. 37:27; Neh. 5:1; Isa. 58:7). Thus, the departure of a man from his parents and his "one flesh" union with his wife indicate the formation of a kinship unit, a family with offspring. In Israel, a man and woman and their children formed a "one flesh" unit in a larger clan/tribal identity of shared bone and flesh.

Several elements related to Eden need brief explication. First, the Hebrew word for "garden" (*gan*) can refer to a cultivated plot of land, but it may also represent a larger expanse— more like a public garden or even a park. What is called the Garden of Eden is actually a part of the area known as Eden. This is the implication of 2:10. Second, Eden and the garden have a precious commodity in its abundant water. The narrator describes a primordial time even before the creation of the garden and before it had rained, when there was subterranean water (2:6). After the creation of the man and the garden, there is no indication when it began to rain in the habitable world.

The next explicit reference to rain in Genesis comes in the account of the flood in Genesis 6–9. Eden's rivers are indispensable for cultivation, whether in the garden or outside it. Third, the garden has two named trees. One is the tree of life, from which the man may eat. Apparently it could sustain human life indefinitely (Genesis 3:22). The man may not eat, however, from the second, the tree of the knowledge of good and evil (2:9, 16). To do so would lead to death—that is, the loss of the breath of life and return to the dust of the ground (3:19). Interpreters debate the significance of the phrase "knowledge of good and evil." Possibly "good and evil" is a merism—that is, a phrase expressing a full range or totality of a subject. The closest parallel expressions in the HB (2 Sam. 14:17, 19:36; 1 Kings 3:9), however, suggest that "knowing" good and evil is more about discernment and proper response among options than it is objective knowledge of a range of data. According to Genesis 3:22, after eating the fruit of the tree, the man and woman were like God (and angels; cf. 2 Sam. 14:17) in knowing good and evil; nevertheless, they remained finite and fallible.

CHARACTERIZATION AND THEME

Here is a partial list of divine actions in 2:4–25:

> Made the earth and the heavens (v. 4)
> Not yet caused it to rain (v. 5)
> Formed the man (v. 7)
> Breathed the breath of life (v. 7)
> Planted a garden (v. 8)
> Made trees grow (v. 9)
> Placed the man in the garden to work (vv. 8, 15)
> Instructed the man on acceptable behavior (vv. 16–17)
> Formed the animals and birds (v. 19)

Brought deep sleep upon the man (v. 21)
Took a rib from the man and made a woman (v. 21).

In this account, the Lord God is frequently the subject of a verb. Several of them are also associated with human activity. Humans, too, make, form, and plant things. Put another way, God's actions in bringing forth a habitable world are described in anthropomorphic terms.

How might we characterize the relationship between God and the man? Although God is not described physically, his interactions with the man are interpersonal. God puts the man in the garden, brings the animals to him, talks directly with him, and to use a modern phrase, performs surgery on him. We might also ask about the proximity of the two in terms of residence. The man lives in the garden, but nothing is said about God's residence. Eden and the garden represent a place of unmediated access to God, or at least a place where God takes the initiative to relate directly to the man and woman.

The man is placed in the garden to work (*'abad*) in it and to keep (*shemer*) it. These common verbs can have various nuances in the HB. On the one hand, the verb *'abad* can have the meaning of tilling and agricultural work (Gen. 4:2, 12); on the other hand, it can refer to the service rendered unto a deity— that is, acts of worship (Exod. 3:12, 20:5; Ps. 100:2). Something similar can be said for the verb *shemer.* It can refer to the agricultural tasks of keeping flocks (Gen. 30:31) and watching over fields (Jer. 4:17) or the religious tasks of keeping such things as commandments (Gen. 26:5), statutes (Lev. 18:4), God's covenant (Exod. 19:5), and one's priestly duties (Num. 3:10). The agricultural connotations of working in and keeping the garden are clear in 2:8, 15; but given the man's completion of them as divinely given tasks, do they perhaps intimate something more? Here we return to the observations above about Eden as a place of access to God. The garden is a part of Eden, where

God is found and where God speaks to and interacts with the humans in it. That same immediacy does not continue in the HB outside of the garden, as the continuation of the narrative in Genesis 3 makes clear.

Some interpreters, drawing on the world behind the text, conclude that Eden represents something of a divine sanctuary, analogous to an ancient temple and its sacred grounds, with the first man and woman serving the Lord God analogously to the priests and worshipers in such a setting. Temples in the ANE were indeed a place where divine presence could be accessed and the service/worship of deities carried out. In various ways earthly temples were representative microcosms of the divine world and the created order willed by the gods. Eden, therefore, could represent a proto-temple and/or the Garden of Eden portray a parklike extension of the Lord God's earthly realm. On the other hand, man and woman in the garden may represent nothing more than the conviction that human beings were created to serve God in the habitable world. This conviction is represented in ancient Mesopotamian texts such as *Atrahasis* and the *Enuma Elish*.

The Lord God brought animals to the man to see what he would call them (2:18–20). Names are important identity markers in the HB,[2] and the man's naming of the animals indicates a role of responsibility in the habitable world. Although both creatures, the narrator has indicated that animals are not a suitable companion for the man. Only the woman, who shares the man's flesh and bone, can form a one-flesh union with him and then bear children. This, too, is a human role of responsibility. The narrator provides an etiology for marriage and family in 2:24, with the comment that a man should leave father and mother and be joined to his wife. This brief creation narrative explains for its Israelite audience how the habitable world came into being. Of all the things that might be said at the conclusion of a story about origins, this one ends with an etiology for the human family, the central human institution in the habitable world.

CONTEXT: THE PREFACE
IN GENESIS 1:1–2:3

The book of Genesis begins with an account of creation in six days and the report that God rested on the seventh day. How does this account relate to that in Genesis 2:4–25, which goes over some of the same ground (pardon the pun)? It is a question of reading our passage in context. Interpreters have discussed this question for centuries. Modern scholars frequently point to the differences between the two accounts, including the suggestion that they represent separate sources now placed together by an editor (cf. the brief comments earlier). More particularly, interpreters have proposed that Genesis 1:1–2:3 originates from a priestly author or circle, while the account in 2:4–25 is from a writer/compiler who used the name Yahweh for God from the beginning of the account. That name for deity is not used 1:1–2:3. Traditionally, the priestly source was thought to be post-exilic in date and the Yahwistic source (or the J source, as it was frequently described), a pre-exilic tradition. In recent years some interpreters have proposed that the Yahwistic source may not be older than the P source. Others have concluded that while multiple traditions underlie the book of Genesis, it is too difficult to identify continuous sources in it and we should think of the book more as the result of repetitive editing and updating. In any case, we have before us two accounts of origins, and our question is: How does the first one introduce or relate to the second one?

Let's look briefly at some of the data in 1:1–2:3 that we may then compare to those in the second account:

God (*'elohim*) created (*bar'a*) the heavens and the earth 1:1

Day 1: God spoke and there was light, and separated it from the darkness 1:3–5

Day 2: God made a dome, separating waters above from those below and named the dome sky 1:6–8

Day 3: God gathered the waters below and earth (*'eres*) appeared. The waters God called seas. The earth produced vegetation and trees of every kind. 1:9–13

Day 4: God made the lights in the sky, including a great one to rule over the day and a lesser one to rule over the night. 1:14–19

Day 5: God created the living creatures of the seas and birds that fly in the sky. 1:20–23

Day 6: God made the animals and then humankind (*'adam*) as male and female in his image. 1:24–31

Day 7: God rested on this day, and blessed it and made it holy. 2:1–3

Genesis 1:1 briefly reports the creation of the heavens and the earth. The narrative that follows provides details according to a seven-day framework. That framework, however, plays no role in the second account, where the only explicit chronological reference is to the "day" when the earth and heavens were made (2:4b). A generic term for deity translated as "God" (*'elohim*) is used throughout the account (35 times). The verb translated as "create" in 1:1 is used consistently in the HB with God as its subject. It is used five times elsewhere in the first account. In the second account, that verb occurs only in the heading (2:4a). To anticipate the discussion that follows, 2:4a may function as a hinge between the two accounts.

The creation of humankind in God's image is summarily reported for Day 6. Comparing its data with the making of the man and woman in the second account is an illuminating exercise. In 1:26 *'adam* occurs without the definite article and is the collective term for humankind, furthered defined as "male" and "female." The terms "man" and "woman"—so central to the etiology in 2:24—may be presumed in the first account, but do not occur in it. Correspondingly, the nouns "male" and "female," do not occur in the second account. And then there is the striking affirmation that humankind is created in God's image and likeness. This affirmation has understandably received a lot of attention from interpreters over the centuries. Suffice it to say here that these terms have a physical and representative function. They can indicate kinship, where children bear the image and likeness of parents as the next generation of humans (e.g., Gen. 5:3). In the ANE, kings symbolically bore the image of deities, and as such, represented them on the earth in carrying out divine instruction. In the context of the Day 6 description, perhaps we can say that humanity is uniquely God's image in the world, representing God as stewards in carrying out the mandates of filling and subduing the habitable world (1:26b–29). This would cohere with the roles for man and woman in Genesis 2 and the etiology of the family. Humankind as male and female, being fruitful and subduing the land, carried out these tasks in kinship units.

Given the differences in vocabulary and detail in the two accounts, one wonders at a final narrator's mindset in putting them together. Did that person, for example, think that the creation of the man and then later the woman in chapter 2 were additional details for the Day 6 summary given in 1:24–31? Was Eden considered part of the Day 3 creation and the planting of a garden there done later (cf. 2:8)? Or are these questions examples of modern linear thinking? Possibly the final narrator was more concerned to put the data at hand before an intended audience and less concerned to coordinate a sequence of events for Genesis 1–2. One indication of the final narrator's intent may be 2:4a. We described it initially as a heading for what follows. It may also function as a hinge between the two accounts, using the verb of divine creation (*bar'a*) from Genesis 1:1 to describe the details of making and forming that follow in the second account. Genesis 1:1–2:3, then, functions as a preface in the sense of a first introduction of matters, which will receive elaboration or additional commentary in what follows in 2:4–25. However we sort out the details, the proximity of the first account of creating a habitable world inevitably influences the way we read the second one.

CONTEXT: THE NARRATIVE CONTINUES IN GENESIS 3

After the creation of the woman, life continues in the garden. The plot thickens, so to speak, with the introduction of a crafty serpent and the expulsion of the human couple from the garden as a result of their disobedience to divine instruction. The world outside of the garden is different from Eden, but it, too, is habitable.

The serpent's "craftiness" (*'arum*, 3:1) is a play on the "nakedness" (*'erom*, 3:7; cf. 2:25) of the man and his wife. He deceives the woman, who eats from the tree of the knowledge of good and evil and gives some of the fruit to her husband. This is the tree in the midst of the garden from which the Lord God had earlier forbidden the man to eat. After eating, the couple realize that their nakedness is a matter of shame and they clothe themselves. The recriminations and assessment of blame in 3:12–13 have occupied interpreters over the centuries, although there is no discussion of them elsewhere in the HB! We will set them aside for the moment and continue with reflecting on man and woman's transition to the post-Eden habitable world.

The serpent's craftiness led the couple to a new perspective on human nakedness, a sign that their knowledge of good and evil had undergone a fundamental change. Not only had their assessment of their nakedness changed but they also feared how the Lord God would respond to their exposure and disobedience. This brings us back to the second creation account, where the man is told that in the day he eats of the tree he shall die (2:17). Death is not further defined in that prohibition, and neither the man nor the woman ceased to exist on the day of their eating from the tree. Life outside of Eden, however habitable, effectively included a death sentence (3:16–24) for the first couple, something passed on to their descendants.

An Israelite audience would see their mortality portrayed in God's announcement regarding the tree (2:17), just as they saw marriage and family portrayed in the etiology of 2:24. Perhaps we can say that the characterization of the man and the woman in the Eden narrative of Genesis 2–3 is essentially etiological in function. Their story is not simply about origins as a past era; it also explains the post-Eden habitable world as the Israelite audience knew it. The curse on the serpent makes it a reptile, as Israel knew the species, enigmatic, dangerous, and crawling in the dust (3:14–15). For the woman, there would be anxiety and pain in conceiving and bearing children, yet her "desire" for her husband would continue (3:16). Contextually, the term "desire" seems to represent a maternal instinct and commitment to the family in spite of the physical toll of childbearing. This aspect of her characterization is reinforced in the report that the man named her Eve, a wordplay on the word for "living" (3:20). The patriarchal structure of ANE society is reflected in the statement that her husband would "rule" over her. The verb (*mashal*) is the same one used to describe the function of the sun and moon, respectively, in defining day and night

(Gen. 1:18). For the man, the ground is cursed so that tilling it for agricultural products is an arduous and never-ending task. He was formed from the ground and in death he will return to it and become dust again (3:17–19).

The Lord God clothed Adam and Eve and sent them out into another habitable—though dangerous—world, where they would be fruitful and where their descendants would learn ways to call upon the Lord's name (Gen. 4:26). The Eden narrative portrays primeval time. It also offered a portrayal of life with the Lord God that could still inform Israel's self-understanding in a post-Eden world, with all its choices of good and evil, and the never-ending task of responding to divine instruction.

10

1 Kings 21

A Royal Family and Its Influence
in Prophetic Perspective

IN 1 KINGS 21, READERS encounter three characters portrayed elsewhere in Kings; and for the first and only time they meet Naboth the Jezreelite. Naboth is mentioned by name elsewhere in Kings—an important matter (see later)—but this is the only narrative in which he appears as a character. The three "known" persons are Ahab, the king of Israel; Jezebel, his wife and queen; and Elijah, the Tishbite, a prophet of the Lord. As always, the task of providing an outline is a handy way to connect the events of the narrative and to begin the process of examining how it says what it says and to what purpose:

I. Ahab offers to purchase a vineyard from
   Naboth   21:1–2
II. Naboth refuses Ahab's offer   21:3
III. Ahab pouts in anger over Naboth's refusal   21:4–6
IV. Jezebel promises to get the vineyard for Ahab   21:7
V. Jezebel plots against Naboth   21:8–14
   A. Sets up false witnesses against Naboth   21:8–10
   B. Naboth convicted of cursing God and
       king   21:11–13a
   C. Naboth executed   21:13b–14

VI. Jezebel encourages Ahab and he acquires the
vineyard   21:15–16

VII. The word of the Lord comes to the prophet
Elijah   21:17–24

A. Ahab and his family will be destroyed   21:17–22

B. Jezebel and others will be eaten by dogs   21:23–24

VIII. A summary negative evaluation of Ahab   21:25–26

IX. Ahab wears sackcloth and fasts   21:27

X. The word of the Lord comes to the prophet
Elijah   21:28–29

A. Ahab has humbled himself   21:28

B. His house will be destroyed in the days of his
son   21:29

The account has two primary parts. The first is a brief presentation of the nefarious way that Ahab acquired Naboth's vineyard (21:1–16), while the second presents the responses of the Lord to the criminal behavior of Ahab and Jezebel (21:17–29). In the second part, Elijah delivers the Lord's responses and the judgment in them is expanded by a diatribe against Ahab (21:25–26).

CONNECTING EVENTS IN THE NARRATIVE AND DISCERNING A THEME

Ahab's proposed property purchase is summarily turned down by Naboth. This results in sullen behavior, which draws the attention of Jezebel. She encourages Ahab with the promise that she will get the vineyard for him. In seven verses, the narrator has presented us with a problem in the royal household, including the repetition of key phrases—a fine example of Hebrew narrative style.

Jezebel writes to the leaders of Naboth's city and instructs them to rig court proceedings against Naboth. Again, in classical narrative style, the narrator describes the public trial, with false testimony that Naboth cursed God and king, and concludes with the report that Naboth was executed. All of this, too, including repetition of key details, comes in just seven verses. We are not given the name of Naboth's city in this account, although it is mentioned twice (vv. 8, 11). Plausibly, it is Jezreel. Ahab had a palace in Jezreel—though Samaria is the royal capital—and Naboth's vineyard is near it. Jezreel is located near the center of a valley in Israel of the same name.

How did Naboth's death open the way for Ahab to acquire his vineyard? The narrator does not provide this detail, either. As readers we might be inclined to think that at his death the vineyard passed on to his relatives. Naboth's response to Ahab seemed decisive—"the Lord forbid that I should give you the inheritance of my fathers" (21:3), something Ahab repeated to Jezebel (v. 4). Perhaps his "treason" (see later) made it possible for Ahab to acquire it. In terms of narrative flow, Ahab travels to the vineyard to take possession of it, assuming his difficulty with Naboth has come to an end with the latter's death. The brevity of the narrative is such that we don't know how Ahab participated in the false charges against Naboth or if he simply acquiesced to Jezebel's plot.

The second part of the chapter is structured around the introductory phrase, "the word of the Lord came to Elijah the Tishbite," which occurs twice (21:17, 28). Elijah is commanded by the Lord to meet Ahab and to charge him with murder and theft. In addition, he is to announce that in the place where Naboth was executed, a place where dogs licked up his blood, dogs will lick up Ahab's blood as well. The role of dogs in eating human flesh and blood is mentioned repeatedly by Elijah, a clear indication to readers that they should look for reoccurrence of these details elsewhere.

Ahab's reply is brief and surprising: "Have you found me, my enemy?" (21:20). Does this mean that Ahab and Elijah know one another? The intended audience (and readers of 1 Kings) knows that they have met before and that other prophets have also confronted Ahab. We'll return to these aspects of the story in the discussion that follows. Elijah replies affirmatively to Ahab with the same verb and proceeds to announce God's judgment upon him, Jezebel, and his people (nation), for their wickedness.

A diatribe against Ahab and Jezebel expands Elijah's words, describing the king as uniquely evil and comparing his idolatry to that of the Amorites—the inhabitants of Canaan at the time of the Israelite settlement in the land (21:25–26). This is an abrupt change in speaker; idolatry is not the same crime as Naboth's murder, and the description sounds like a general summary of his reign. Indeed, one could remove these two verses from the second section of the chapter and it would then primarily comprise dialogue between prophet and king. Some translations, therefore, put these verses in parenthesis (e.g., ESV, NRSV), concluding that they are an editorial comment or material that the narrator has added to the dialogue between king and prophet.

Ahab also responds by donning sackcloth and fasting. The word of the Lord then comes a second time to Elijah, announcing that in light of Ahab's humbling himself, the disaster announced against him will fall instead on Ahab's "house" during the days of his son. This concluding comment explains that Ahab's death will not bring the rule of his house to an end. It is also another detail in the account that urges readers to continue with the longer portrayal of the Omride Dynasty in 1 and 2 Kings.

Have we discerned a theme in 1 Kings 21 in the analysis of the narrative's flow? Perhaps there is more than one! Here is a proposal: the Lord will bring judgment on the wickedness of Ahab and his house.

CHARACTERIZATION AND POINT OF VIEW

How is Ahab portrayed? We have his actions and speaking (the two primary ways of characterization in Hebrew narratives), plus the summary evaluation of him by an editor. One element that stands out is his reaction to Naboth's refusal. His "resentful and sullen" (NRSV) description in verse 4 seems like modern psycho-social analysis! A check of a concordance (English or Hebrew) shows that Ahab is the only person so described with this word pair and that it is used of him one other time in 1 Kings 20:35–43, when he is confronted by an unnamed prophet and the king goes "resentful and sullen" to his palace in Samaria. The Hebrew concordance will show additionally that Jezebel uses one of the two terms (*sar* in Hebrew) in talking with Ahab in 21:5. The NRSV translates it as "depressed."

Ahab pouts to the extent that he won't even eat! Jezebel goads him with a reminder that he is king of Israel, even as she promises to get him the vineyard. He speaks only briefly to the prophet and then engages in acts of repentance. The narrator prepares readers for Ahab's death, which comes in the next chapter.

Jezebel is more active than Ahab and is the instigator of perjury, murder, and theft. She embodies the proverbial phrase of "power behind the throne." Her murderous threat to Elijah in a prior story (1 Kings 19:1–2) is stronger than Ahab's description of Elijah as an enemy in 21:20. Modern readers may see the relationship between Jezebel and Ahab as pathologically enabling and co-dependent. The narrator presents it as cause for Israel's failure and the impetus for prophetically announced divine judgment. In her instructions to the leaders in Naboth's city, Jezebel asked that he be accused of "cursing God and king" (21:9). These are heinous charges and result in capital punishment. The charge of cursing the king may also reflect Jezebel's cunning in thwarting Naboth's family claim to the land. Her husband is an aggrieved party and plausibly could take the property as recompense. Elsewhere there is mention of the blood of Naboth's sons, suggesting that they, too, were executed (2 Kings 9:26) as a result of Naboth's conviction. One wonders about the collusion between the officials of Naboth's city and the royal house. Such a question is not related per se to Jezebel's characterization, except to say that she exploited a means to a murderous end.

Naboth is a good example of a minor character, who is nevertheless an important figure in the account and a person remembered years later when Jezebel and Ahab's son Joram are killed (2 Kings 9:24–37). He speaks a single sentence and dies without a word spoken on his behalf at trial. It is difficult to know the extent to which the narrator has pared down source material to underscore the primary goal of exposing Ahab and Jezebel's guilt.

"In the place where dogs licked up Naboth's blood, dogs will lick up your blood—indeed yours!" (21:19). There is symmetry claimed between the "place" of Naboth's tragic fate and Ahab's postmortem humiliation. That place is described simply as outside of Naboth's city (21:13) and designated as the location of divine reckoning for Ahab. Naboth's property (a different place from the site of his execution?) will come back to play a role in the death of Jezebel and his son Joram (2 Kings 9:24–37).

How does Ahab die? Literarily speaking, it comes quickly in the next chapter, although the narrative lists three years of elapsed time. He dies of a wound incurred in battle with the

Aramaeans at Ramoth Gilead east of the Jordan River (1 Kings 22:29–38). The details, such as they are, suggest the king bled to death in his chariot. His body was taken to Samaria, where he was buried. The narrator concludes the battle account with the following report: "They washed out the chariot at the pool in Samaria. The dogs licked up his blood where prostitutes bathed themselves, according to the word the Lord had spoken" (v. 38). Surprisingly, given Elijah's earlier prophecy and the link to it in verse 38, the place of the macabre scene is Samaria. Does this mean that Naboth was executed near Samaria and not Jezreel? Or does it suggest that the report in verse 38 depends on alternative traditions of Ahab's demise?

However we assess the report of Ahab's death, we need to follow the literary lead in Elijah's prophecies, where dogs are twice mentioned as consuming human remains from Ahab's house (21:23–24, 29). This will bring us again to Naboth and other members of Ahab's family. Upon his death, Ahab was succeeded by two sons; the first was Ahaziah, and when he died, Joram[1] ascended the throne. These three, along with Omri, the founder of the dynasty, ruled over Israel some forty-eight years. During this time, Elisha succeeded Elijah in his prophetic tasks, including the anointing of an Israelite army officer named Jehu to bring judgment upon the "house of Ahab" and to be Israel's next king (2 Kings 9:1–10). Joram is killed and his body is thrown contemptuously in the field of Naboth the Jezreelite. Jehu cites a prophecy that the Lord would repay the blood of Naboth *and his sons* in the field belonging to Naboth (2 Kings 9:25–26). As indicated briefly, this report offers readers additional perspective on the way in which Ahab acquired Naboth's property, here called a portion of a field rather than a vineyard. If his sons were executed along with him or subsequently, it would make it simpler to transfer Naboth's property to the aggrieved party. There is no mention of dogs in Naboth's field.

We should note that the presentation of Jezebel's death in 2 Kings 9:30–37 also draws on Elijah's prophecy of judgment in 21:23. She is thrown out of a window in Jezreel, and after her death only portions of her body were found. Jehu describes this as a fulfillment of Elijah's words that "on the plot of ground in Jezreel dogs will eat the flesh of Jezebel." As with Ahab's death, there are also differences in detail with her death when compared to Elijah's words in 21:23. The common element in their deaths is dogs partaking of human remains.

How might we characterize Elijah in chapter 21? Here are two observations that, like the details of Naboth's portrayal, will lead us to see the account in a larger literary and thematic context. Elijah is summoned by the Lord to confront Ahab. First, the confrontation appears to take place at Naboth's vineyard, but the setting takes a back seat to the content of Elijah's prophecy. Second, his prophetic speech is rhetorically formulaic. Twice we read that "the word of the Lord came to Elijah" and twice the content of the prophecies is prefaced with the phrase "thus says the Lord." A quick check of a concordance shows that both phrases occur frequently in the HB. The first is used over a hundred times and refers to the reception of divine revelation (e.g., Ezek. 1:3). The second occurs over four hundred times and introduces the content of divine revelation to an audience (e.g., Isa. 43:1). It is based on the importance of messenger speech in the ANE, where appointed figures speak on behalf of those who send them by indicating the sender in an introductory phrase (e.g., Gen. 32:4). Both phrases are used elsewhere in 1 Kings to describe Elijah's prophetic activity (e.g., 17:2, 14; cf. Jer. 2:1, 5). Elijah's role, therefore, in 1 Kings 21 is quintessentially prophetic. Much about him recedes into the background in 1 Kings 21, while the content of his prophecies and their divine warrant take center stage.

THEME AND MOTIF
IN CONTEXT(S)

Ahab's characterization as "resentful and sullen" in verse 4 is an echo from the scene prior to the Naboth affair, where he had been confronted by an unnamed prophet (20:43). Elijah's portrayal in chapter 21, then, is another example of a "confronting prophet" motif, reinforcing God's assessment of Ahab's culpability from one scene to another. Indeed, Ahab has several encounters with prophets in 1 Kings. The two lists that follow reflect the motif of the prophet encountering kings and army commanders in 1 and 2 Kings. Those with a single asterisk* are confrontive/judgmental in message; those with a double asterisk** contain prophecies against Ahab and/or his family.

Elijah	17:1–2*
Elijah	18:1–45*
Unnamed prophets	20:13–14, 22, 28, 35–43*/**
Elijah	21:17–29*/**
Micaiah, son of Imlah	22:7–28*/**

Moreover, after Ahab's death his sons and other rulers have them in 2 Kings:

Elijah	Ahaziah's messengers and soldiers	1:3–17*/**
Elisha	Joram and Jehoshaphat	3:11–19
Elisha	Naaman, Aramaean commander	5:4–19
Elisha	Joram and his messengers	6:32–7:2
Elisha	Hazael, Aramaean general and king	8:7–13**
Elisha	Jehu, Israelite commander and king	9:1–9**

Even a cursory glance at 1 Kings 17–2 Kings 10 shows that these are not the only accounts of prophetic activity during the Omride era. The portrayal of the dynasty abounds with stories of prophetic figures, so that some interpreters can refer to this section of Kings as the Elijah–Elisha cycle. These data thus situate 1 Kings 21 in related literary contexts. In its immediate context, the account is sandwiched between two narratives of battles with the Aramaeans, with prophetic encounters and judgment against Ahab common to all three. The prophetic judgments on his house, furthermore, have echoes and connections throughout the portrayal of the Omride Dynasty. This is point-of-view selectivity and shaping at work to construct a larger plot and accentuate a theme.

Something similar can be said about selectivity in Naboth's portrayal. The shaping of the data about him resulted in some unanswered questions. As a Jezreelite, his connection to Jezreel is not clearly defined, except for the location of his property near to it. The deaths of Ahab, Jezebel, and Joram, however, are all linked to Naboth's as poetic justice. This is Naboth's role in the larger narrative.

We can (and should) extend this exploration of context by asking about the plot and purpose of 1 and 2 Kings. Space allows only a cursory treatment. The books of Kings portray Israelite and Judahite history over a period of some four centuries. The chronology contained in them is keyed to the years of royal rule, as the national story unfolded from the last days of King David to the captivity of King Jehoiachin in Babylon. The state of Israel ruled by David and Solomon split into the kingdoms of Israel and Judah (1 Kings 1–12); a period of parallel states is brought to an end with the defeat of Israel by the Neo-Assyrians (1 Kings 13–2 Kings 17); Judah continues as a state until its defeat by the Neo-Babylonians (2 Kings 18–25). The story told by Kings, therefore, concludes with portions of Israel and Judah's population dispersed in the ANE and Babylonian control over the lands of Israel and Judah. How and why did the people of God go from a nation-state led by David, God's anointed ruler, through political disintegration, to loss of their autonomy? The books of Kings answer these related questions (and others!).

The portrayal of the house of Ahab during the period of the parallel states is central to answering the "how" and "why" questions of the longer narrative. Omri, the dynasty's founder, gets only a few verses, while Ahab, Jezebel, and his sons are prominent characters in 1 Kings 16:29–2 Kings 10:17. More space is devoted in the Kings narratives to the house of Ahab than to any other dynasty in the separate state of Israel. Moreover, it receives more attention than the rulers in Judah during the same period. We can contrast this literary profile with the way the chronicler portrays the same period, where Jehoshaphat and other Judahite rulers receive the majority of attention (2 Chron. 17:1–22:9).

Ahab is introduced in 1 Kings 16:29b–30 as follows: "Ahab son of Omri reigned over Israel in Samaria twenty-two years. Ahab son of Omri did evil in the sight of the LORD more than all who were before him" (NRSV). This introduction is followed by an initial report that Ahab was sinful like a previous Israelite king named Jeroboam, that he married Jezebel, a Sidonian (Phoenician) princess, and that he built a temple for the deity Baal in Samaria (1 Kings 16:31–34). It contains another summary evaluation that "Ahab did more to provoke the Lord than all the Israelite kings before him." Here is the art of explanation and persuasion at work. How similar these summary statements are to the diatribe in 1 Kings 21:24–25. What we read in 1 Kings 21, then, is one account of the larger portrait of a failed monarch, whose sinfulness led not only to his demise but that of Israel as well.

In the summary explanation of Israel's fall to the Assyrians, the narrator states that the Lord had warned Israel by every prophet and seer, but to no avail (2 Kings 17:13–14, 22–23). The portrayal of Ahab's house corresponds to this explanation. Later in the Kings narrative, the wickedness of Manasseh, king of Judah, is described as decisive for the failure of Judah and its subsequent fall to the Babylonians (21:1–16, 24:1–4). Like Ahab, Manasseh shed innocent blood and was an idolater. The narrator explains Manasseh's wickedness by reporting that he would be judged with the measuring line of Samaria and the plummet of the house of Ahab (21:13; cf. Mic. 6:16).

In chapter 1 we noted that 1 and 2 Kings are considered by many modern interpreters as part of a larger Deuteronomistic History, the last component in a collection that tells the story of Israel from its entrance into the land of Canaan through the defeat of Judah at the hands of the Babylonians. The point of view in composition, the development of plot and theme, and the summary evaluative comments in Kings may well be the work of ancient historians also involved in producing the other books in the collection. That would expand even further the exercise of a contextual reading of 1 Kings 21.

1 KINGS 21 AND THE WORLD BEHIND THE TEXT

Let's first explore briefly the relationship of point of view and theme to historical context. We suggested that 1 and 2 Kings respond to the questions of how and why the people of God failed and were judged by God in the historical process. The narrative concludes with the people of God in exile, and this is the likely setting for the compiler(s) of Kings, who fashioned written (cf. 1 Kings 16:27) and oral materials into a national history. Possibly he/they reworked a previous national history by updating it after the fall of Jerusalem. The stories about an evil Ahab could have coalesced in response to the defeat and dispersion of Israel in the latter part of the eighth century BCE and then were reframed in light of Judah's later downfall. As with the discussion of the book of Ruth, where proposals about the setting of the writer(s) and the intended audience influence the conclusions of its purpose, so it is with 1 and 2 Kings. Those vitally interested in persuading an audience, not disinterested reporters, produced this form of a national history.

There are written sources from the ANE that refer to Ahab and his house, with intriguing data to compare with the portrayal in Kings:

1. In the annals of Shalmaneser III, Ahab is named as one of the leaders of a military coalition of twelve kings opposing Assyrian encroachment in the region. The battle took place at the North Syrian site of Qarqar. Historians date the battle to 853 BCE. This edition of Shalmaneser's annals was inscribed on a stone monolith discovered at Kurkh in southeastern Turkey. We should note that Shalmaneser campaigned repeatedly in the eastern Mediterranean during his long reign (858–824 BCE). Here is the segment naming Ahab:

> I approached the city of Qarqar. I razed, destroyed and burned the city of Qarqar, his [Qarqar's ruler] royal city. 1,200 chariots, 1,200 calvary, and 20,000 troops of Hadad-ezer of Damascus, 700 chariots of chariots, 700 cavalry, and 10,000 troops of Irhuleni, the Hamathite; 2,000 chariots, and 10,000 troops of Ahab, the Israelite. . . . [T]hese 12 kings he took as his allies. (COS II, 263–64)

Nothing of Ahab fighting against Shalmaneser is portrayed in 1 Kings, although the coalition would have been a significant commitment on Ahab's part. Shalmaneser also claims tribute from Jehu in another monolithic inscription, where he is described as from the "house of Omri" (COS II, 270).[2] This is not mentioned, either, in 2 Kings. The compilers of Kings were interested in other matters. Note that the Aramaean king Hadad-ezer is a partner with Ahab in opposing the Assyrians. Ahab fights the Aramaeans repeatedly in 1 Kings 20 and 22, whose king is

Ben Hadad. Interpreters debate whether the dynastic name "Ben Hadad," which was used by more than one king of Damascus, represents the Hadad-ezer of Shalmaneser's Annals.

2. The Moabite king Mesha (2 Kings 3:4) produced an inscription of some thirty-four lines that describes his reign, which included a time of subjugation to Israel under Omri and his son. It was found in Dhiban (ancient Dibon) in Jordan. He claims defeat of Israel through several battles and provides a list of building accomplishments. The inscription is retrospective of his reign and is dated circa 835 BCE. Here is the portion naming Omri and his son:

> Omri was the king of Israel, and he oppressed Moab for many days, for Kemosh was angry with his land. And his son succeeded him, and he said—he too—"I will oppress Moab!" In my days did he say [so], but I looked down on him and on his house, and Israel has gone to ruin, yes, it has gone to ruin for ever! And Omri had taken possession of the whole land of Medeba, and he lived there his days and half the days of his son, forty years, but Kemosh restored it in my days. (COS II, 137)

Interpreters differ whether the second reference to Omri's "son" refers to Ahab or Joram, since 2 Kings 3:1–27 indicate that Mesha rebelled against Israel after Ahab died. The Moabite word could refer to either son or descendant. However one sorts out the chronology of Mesha's rebellion, the Moabite king describes a dominating presence of Israel in Moab during Omri's reign and at least part of Ahab's tenure, if not longer. The reference to Israel's "ruin" is hyperbolic, but it likely presupposes the death of Joram and the subjugation of Jehu to Assyria.

3. A fragmentary Aramaic inscription discovered at Tel Dan in northern Israel refers to a king of Israel at least twice

and provides a portion of an Israelite royal name. The inscription was apparently written by an Aramaean ruler, who refers to the killing of an Israelite king, among other exploits. Unfortunately the ruler's name is not preserved and only the last two consonants (*rm*) of the Israelite king's name are preserved. The inscription dates to approximately the same time as that of Mesha. Some interpreters think that the Israelite king is Joram, Ahab's son. Here is a reconstruction and translation of the relevant portion. The brackets represent broken space in the stone fragments and scholars offer various proposals to fill them:

> I killed kin[gs] who harnessed . . . [ch]ariots and thousands of horsemen . . . [ ]rm son of [ ] king of Israel and kill[ed]yahu son of [I ovrthr]ew the house of David. (COS II, 161–62)

In 2 Kings 9:14–29, Jehu kills Joram son of Ahab and Ahaziah son of Jehoram, king of Judah. One way to read this Aramaic inscription is to see the second line restored as "[Jo]ram son of [Ahab] and kill[ed Ahaz]yahu son Jehoram]." The "house of David" would be a dynastic reference to the kingdom of Judah. Ahaziah is the English spelling of Ahazyahu. If this reconstruction is correct, it raises interesting questions for the claims in 2 Kings 9 that Jehu killed Joram and had his body discarded in Naboth's property.

Finally, here are some brief historical and cultural observations on items of interest in 1 Kings 21.

1. *Jezreel and Samaria.* The ruins from both sites have been partially excavated, providing some information about their function in ancient Israel. An up-to-date, multivolume Bible dictionary will provide a good overview of what is known about them from ancient literary and historical sources, such

excavation reports. Generally speaking, the material culture for the mid-ninth century BCE and the time of the Omrides is the most developed of any during the broader Israelite period (Iron Age II). Large cities like Hazor and Megiddo reached the pinnacle of their architectural development during the Omride period, including what are very likely stables for the chariot corps. As befits the capital, Samaria had ashlar masonry construction, administrative/public buildings, and furniture inlaid with ivory. All these are signs of wealth and prestige. Jezreel was a fortified regional city with towers on its walls. It watched over the eastern half of the Jezreel Valley (a rich agricultural area) and approaches to the Israelite heartland from the Jordan Valley.

2. *Land Tenure and Inheritance.* In light of our discussions of the book of Ruth, we can say that tribal and agrarian culture sought to conserve its property. A major portion of the book of Joshua is dedicated to defining tribal inheritance (13:1–22:9). The land tenure instructions in the Torah are partial, but consistent with this conservative ethos. According to Leviticus 25:23–24, the Lord is the real owner of Israel's land; the people are sojourners in it, and they should maintain "their" property in service to God and their descendants. Naboth's statement that "the Lord forbid that I sell the inheritance of my fathers" fits this ethos. The instructions in the Torah do not, however, reckon with the power of a monarch to override tribal custom and communal agrarian practices (cf. 1 Sam. 8:14). Furthermore, land-retention objectives stand in tension with certain commercial practices, more prevalent in urban areas and stratified societies, where land can be used as valuable capital and purchased without regard to the tribal status of the buyer. Interpreters debate whether Naboth's refusal to sell his inheritance reflects customary law that could stand against an offer from the king, or it is a "traditional" response intended

to impede a superior power, who in both theory and practice could eventually force a transaction from him.

3. *Queens and Their Roles.* The mothers of Judahite kings are regularly listed in the books of Kings, but no royal wife is called "the queen" (*malkah*). That term is used for foreigners like the Queen of Sheba (1 Kings 10:1), although "queen" is customarily used in English to describe a royal wife. Royal wives and mothers of rulers could be called "Great Lady" (*gebirah*), sometimes translated as "Queen Mother." Kings were typically polygamous, so that royal duties could be distributed to different wives or vested in the mother(s) of male heirs, and so on. Royal wives in the ANE were typically drawn from influential families in the realm and the royal houses of neighboring states. Thus their influence could be immense.

Jezebel was the daughter of a Phoenician king (1 Kings 16:31; cf. 2 Kings 9:34). The Phoenician city-states were commercial centers with extensive maritime and overland trading connections. Historians note that during the ninth century BCE, the Phoenicians were in a period of expansion. For example, the traditional date of the founding of Carthage in North Africa, a Phoenician trading colony, is 814 BCE. Likely the marriage of Ahab to Jezebel was part of a lucrative alliance between Phoenicia and Israel. The Kings narratives do not reflect on this alliance, except to oppose Jezebel's patronage of the deities Baal and Asherah.

4. *Criminal Trial.* Criminal trials were typically part of the administrative structure of a village or city, where the elders and local officials had the roles of judge and jury. Ruth 4:1–12 is an example of a noncriminal court gathering, where elders were "witnesses" to a transaction. They did not decide anything. According to Deuteronomy 16:18–20, there should be

judges and officials appointed in all towns to carry out justice. In practice, these responsibilities typically fell to the traditional leaders, even if in cooperation with a state administration that overlay local patterns. An Israelite municipal "official" might have several responsibilities, based on his local status and connections to the royal administration. There was also a type of appeals court for difficult cases, where a judge and a priest had jurisdiction (Deut. 17:8–13). Presumably this court was located in Jerusalem and Israel likely had something similar during the divided monarchy. Apparently the "elders and officials" who received Jezebel's instructions to set up a trial were some or all of the judge(s) and jury. There is no mention of either judge or priest in the proceedings.

The charge against Naboth was blasphemy. It was a capital offense and he was stoned to death (cf. Lev. 24:10–16). Two witnesses were required for a criminal conviction (Deut. 19:15) and two testified falsely against him. They were the mirror image of Exodus 23:1, which militates against false reports and malicious witnesses. Naboth was also charged with cursing the king. This is treason and was possibly included as a charge to make it easier for the aggrieved party (Ahab) to acquire his property in judgment.

Section IV

THE WORLD IN
FRONT OF THE TEXT

11

Reception History
and Classical Stories

*A crucial feature of human life is its fundamentally dialogical char-
acter. It is universally recognized—by developmental psychologists,
social scientists, and philosophers alike—that identity is dialogically
formed. People define their identity always in dialogue with, and
sometimes in struggle against, the things that others see in them.*

EUNNY P. LEE[1]

WHAT MS. LEE SAYS ABOUT dialogical character is directly
applicable to biblical narratives in their conception, composition for an audience, and then reception by later readers. We
have proposed that narratives in the HB are a central way that
Israel rendered an account of itself. The narratives did not arise
in a vacuum! In rendering portions of a national story, authors
both engaged and constructed a world through the material
that they inherited, seeking to explain God's work in that world
and to persuade their audience of its relevancy for their identity.
Subsequent readers, who look over the shoulders of the Israelite
intended audience, engage the biblical narratives dialogically
through the medium of their own experience. This has been
a primary function of the HB—that is, its canonical role—for
the religious communities of Judaism and Christianity, and is
a contributing factor in Islam. And as such, it has also had the
role of a cultural classic in Western society. In what follows, we
look at some examples of reception history in biblical interpretation that is, the ways in which later readers have engaged

biblical narrative. In doing so, we will revisit some characters and narratives.

ABRAHAM, SARAH, ISAAC, HAGAR, AND ISHMAEL

The reception history for Abraham is as broad and rich as that for any other religious figure from the ancient world, owing in large part to the sheer number of people over the centuries who recognize him as a central figure in their religious heritage. The narratives about him in the book of Genesis cast their influence on Judaism, Christianity, and Islam. The impact of those ancestral narratives, therefore, offers superb examples of responses by later audiences.

We begin by noting that responses to the ancestral narratives are something one encounters in the HB itself. Here is one example: an exilic prophet presenting a divine oracle draws on the narrative traditions of Abraham and Sarah and how they went from a childless status to become the ancestors of Israel (Isa. 51:1b–2):

> Look to the rock from which you were quarried and to the source which produced you; Look to Abraham your father and to Sarah who bore you; for Abraham was just one when I called him, but I blessed him and made him numerous.

This poetic allusion reflects on several aspects of the storyline in Genesis 12–26, in the context of the tragic circumstances of the defeat of Judah and the forced migration of some of its inhabitants into exile. What kind of future would there be for defeated Judah and the depopulated, largely ruined city of Jerusalem? These circumstances (and that question) are part of the world behind the text of Isaiah 40–55; and as such, they are also the lens, the world in front of the ancestral stories, through which the prophet of the exile sees them and their relevance for rebuilding a national life. Just as God was true to the promise of progeny for Abraham and Sarah through difficult trials, so God would make Judah and Jerusalem whole communities in the future.

New Testament Adaptations

There are numerous references and allusions to Abraham and Sarah in the New Testament. For example, the Gospel according to Matthew begins with a genealogy of forty-two generations, headed by the introductory comment: "[this is] an account of the genealogy of Jesus Christ, the son of David, the son of Abraham." Abraham is then the first person in the genealogical list (1:1–2). Abraham is understood as the "father" of the Israelites—that is, a defining ancestor (cf. John 8:33; Luke 16:19–31). One central question that early Jewish Christians needed to answer was that of Jesus's identity according to Israel's authoritative writings. The genealogical line provided by Matthew runs from Abraham through David and the kings descended from him, presenting Jesus as David's greater son and thus Israel's Messiah. Indeed, apart from its Christian application, this genealogy is Jewish narrative theology at work. We should note that Tamar (Gen. 38) and Ruth are two of four women included in this genealogy. Rahab and Uriah's wife—that is, Bath-sheba—are the others. "Why these four?" is a fascinating question! Perhaps they illustrate the conviction that God had used women before whose marital status and/or sexual history raised questions. Those who questioned Mary's story, therefore, were going against examples from the canonical storyline. Some of these women, if not all of them, were Gentiles. Perhaps their stories illustrate the conviction that not only is Jesus the Messiah of Israel but he is also the king and savior of nations (cf. Matt. 28:18–20). In any case, the genealogical references to Abraham, Tamar, Rahab, Boaz, and Ruth are preserved to buttress the conclusion that God's work in Israel culminates in the coming of the Messiah and the emergence of the Christian Church.

Abraham's children and the stories behind them are alluded to in the New Testament, but only Isaac is named. He is the child of promise (Rom. 9:6–9), a claim that Paul makes with quotations from Genesis 18:10 and 14, and 21:12. This last reference differentiates Isaac from Ishmael, also Abraham's son. In an allegorical illustration to the Galatians, Paul continues this contrast; in this instance, he contrasts Sarah with Hagar as women figuratively representing two covenants (4:21–31). Again, Paul quotes explicitly from the story of Hagar and Ishmael (Gen. 21:10) and encourages the Galatian Christians to identify with Sarah and Isaac. Earlier in the letter he describes God's promise to bless the nations through Abraham as "proclaiming the Gospel beforehand" (Gal. 3:8; cf. Gen. 12:3, 22:18). He tells the Romans, furthermore, that "God did not spare his son, but gave him up for us" alluding to the dramatic story of Isaac's near sacrifice in Genesis 22 (Rom. 9:33; cf. Heb. 11:17–19).

These brief examples illustrate some ways that the ancestral stories in Genesis (and Ruth and 2 Samuel) contributed to the identity of early Christians. Those accounts were formative for Israelite and Jewish identity, and that meant they were also formative for the Gospel writers and Paul.

Adaptations in the Quran and Islamic Tradition

In our previous examination of Genesis 16 and 21 (chapter 2), we noted the common element of Hagar and Ishmael's struggle to find water in the wilderness. In both accounts an angel assists them in finding it. Beer Lahai Roi is the name of the well in 16:14, a detail which we noted is a wordplay on the encounter with the angel, as well as an etiological reference to explain the significance of the well for later readers. A central story in Islamic tradition tells of Hagar and Ishmael's struggle to find water in the wilderness and how God (Allah) provided a way for them to find it at the well of Zamzam. There are several versions of this story in Muslim tradition, although it is not contained in the Quran. The story, however, is related to the presentation in the Quran that Abraham and Ishmael (Ibrahim and Ismail in Arabic) traveled in the Hejaz region of the Arabian subcontinent, where they built the Kaaba, the sacred shrine in Mecca, still encompassed in the sacred mosque there. Here is the brief portrayal of their building work in the Quran's second chapter (Sura):

> Remember Abraham and Ishmael raised the foundations of the house: "Our Lord accept (this service) from us; for you are the all-hearing, the all-knowing."
>
> "Our Lord make of us Muslims, bowing to your (will), and of our progeny a people Muslim, bowing to your (will); and show us our places for the celebration of rites; and turn unto us (in mercy); for you are the oft-returning, most merciful." (2.127–28, translation of Abdullah Yusuf Ali, slightly modified)

The "house" is the Kaaba. Abraham and Ishmael worked together to build it and their prayer is that God would make them and their descendants to be Muslims. The shrine was not only a place of worship but it also became a place of pilgrimage for Muslims during the last years of Muhammad's life (d. 630 CE), as it remains to this day a central aspect of Muslim identity. Two small hills, Safa and Marwa, are close by, which many current worshipers also visit and encircle (2.158), as is the well of Zamzam, now a short walk from the Kaaba within the courtyard of the sacred mosque in Mecca. The well is not named in the Quran.

Let's go back to Hagar and Ishmael. Muslim tradition holds that when they needed water, Hagar sought it in the arid area of the Mecca valley, looking for it on both hills until God assisted them and they found the water of Zamzam. In most forms of the tradition, it was the angel Gabriel who brought forth the water from the ground. Gabriel is also the angel who first revealed Allah's words to Muhammad.

The Muslim story of Hagar, Ishmael, and the well of Zamzam has obvious connections with those in Genesis 16 and 21. All three stories have the same two characters associated with a water source in the wilderness, where God comes to their aid and the child grows up to be an influential leader in the region. In two of them, Hagar and Ishmael struggle to find water; and in two of them, the name of the well is given. There are, of course, differences between the stories. The location in the valley of Mecca in Muslim versions is different from the settings in the Genesis accounts, which do not have Abraham living in the Arabian subcontinent. The name of the well is also different. On the one hand, we can say that more than a shared motif is evidenced in comparing accounts. The Muslim versions share not only the motif of divine sustenance in the wilderness with the biblical narratives but the same two persons as well. Hagar is not mentioned by name in the Quran, so that her identity as Ishmael's mother and Abraham's wife (or concubine) in Muslim tradition is drawn from the Genesis stories. On the other hand, the Muslim versions are not supplementing or conflating the two biblical accounts. They have adopted two biblical characters and adapted two biblical stories to their own end.

One can see something similar at work in Sura 37.99–113, which portrays Abraham's vision of a near sacrifice of his son. Non-Muslim readers will think of the earlier, dramatic narrative in Genesis 22, where Abraham nearly offers Isaac as a sacrifice in the land of Moriah before the Lord intervenes and provides an acceptable substitute. And indeed, when comparing the two accounts, we see they have obvious connections. They share the motif of the obedient father willing to sacrifice a son, but spared by God from doing so. In the Quranic version, Abraham's son is not named, but it is assumed in Muslim interpretation that it is Ishmael, not Isaac, whom Abraham envisioned sacrificing. Where did it take place? The allusiveness of the Quran does not identify the place, but many Muslim interpreters assume that it was near Mecca. Some, for example, think of the hill of Marwa, mentioned earlier. They interpret the Quranic passage in accordance with the fundamental claim that Abraham and Ishmael built the Kaaba and thus seek to coordinate the vision of a near sacrifice with it.

A close reading of the Genesis 22 account shows that it, too, is related to a central place of worship. God provided a ram as an acceptable substitute for Isaac, so "Abraham named that place 'the Lord will provide,' as it is said to this day, 'on the hill of the Lord, it shall be provided'" (22:14). With this remark, the narrator makes an etiological comment, connecting Abraham's naming of the site with worship on God's mount. More specifically, it connects Abraham's sacrificial worship with that later conducted at the temple in Jerusalem, located on the hill of the Lord. A similar connection is made by the chronicler, who notes that Solomon built the house of the Lord on Mount Moriah, where the Lord had appeared to his father David (2 Chron. 3:1).

The Quran is a remarkably allusive text in the many ways that it draws upon Jewish and Christian traditions. In the book of Genesis, Abraham is called the father of many nations (17:4). And he is connected to the peoples east and south of Canaan through Ishmael (25:12–18). Islam assumes these traditions and expands on them. Over time, Ishmael became known as the father of the Arabs and he is considered the link between Abraham and the early Arab Muslim community. In their reformulating of stories about Abraham and Ishmael, neither the Quran nor Muslim tradition denigrates Isaac in the process. He is recognized as a prophet and the ancestor of the Jews.

The Quran affirms that God gave the Jews a Torah through Moses, but the Torah contained in the HB is not a faithful version of that revelation, since it contains both truth and error. The Quran and Muslim tradition, therefore, are the authoritative interpretation of the ancestral stories about Abraham, Ishmael, and Moses. Muhammad is understood as the seal of prophetic revelation and the culmination of what God had revealed earlier to Jews and then to Christians. Islam and Arabia are two of the lenses (or facets of a diamond) through which to portray the ancestral stories as contributions to yet another religious community.

RUTH, ORPAH, AND BOAZ IN POST-BIBLICAL JEWISH WRITINGS

The book of Ruth offers numerous illustrations of reception history. We'll look briefly at Jewish and rabbinic sources dating to the period 200 CE–900 CE. A primary repository of rabbinic interpretation for the book is the Midrash commonly referred to as Ruth Rabbah. It re-presents the story of Ruth, interspersing the received Hebrew text with homiletical, cultural, and historical comments. Indeed, that re-presenting activity is one way to describe the genre of midrash, a common form of literature in post-biblical Judaism.

In Ruth Rabbah, Ruth's Moabite identity is dealt with through the lenses of Torah interpretation, Jewish communal practices, and kinship with King David. Her kinship with

David also means that she is related to the Jewish Messiah to come (RR 7:4). In the expansive retelling of the story, the conversation between Ruth and Naomi on the way to Bethlehem includes important matters of Jewish identity, such as visiting synagogues, keeping Sabbath regulations, modesty, and avoidance of idolatry (RR 2:22–24). The Targum of Ruth (1:16), an Aramaic paraphrase and expansion of the biblical story, even has Naomi reminding Ruth that there are 613 commandments in Scripture. The biblical narrative itself indicates that Ruth embraced the Yahwistic faith of Israel, but rabbinic interpretation of the story made Ruth's conversion to Judaism central to its re-presenting of the story. She is a Gentile proselyte who embraces Judaism as it was formulated in the rabbinic period. There were no synagogues, for example, during the period of the Judges or the later time of Ruth's composition, but they were central to Jewish identity of the period of the midrashes and targums. Ruth also demonstrates her facility with Torah by informing Boaz that she knows Moabites are excluded from the assembly of the Lord (Deut. 23:3–6). In fine rabbinic fashion, Boaz replies that the prohibition refers to men, thus opening the possibility of her inclusion in the Jewish community (RR 4:1).

Eventually the book of Ruth became a fixed reading at the Jewish festival of Weeks, one of the three pilgrimage festivals mandated in Torah (Lev. 23:15–22). Greek-speaking Jews called it Pentecost. The regularized reading of Ruth at the festival of Weeks is likely a post-Talmudic development, regardless of how far back the practice may have been for some Jews. The Babylonian Talmud is dated circa 500 CE, includes the Mishnah (ca. 200 CE), and draws on accumulated Jewish lore. Since the biblical story of Ruth's gleanings is set in the barley and wheat harvests (2:23), during which the festival is held, the connection between book and festival has some cogency. By this time in the development of the Jewish festival (ca. 500–600 CE), two elements stand out. One is the agricultural connection of giving thanks for the spring harvests; the other is the celebration of the giving of the Torah at Mount Sinai. The reading of the book of Ruth intersects with both in post-biblical Judaism. Regarding God's gift of the Torah, Ruth becomes the celebrated Gentile proselyte, who accepted the yoke of the Torah, and who is a forerunner of Gentiles who will come in the latter days to receive Torah instruction from the Lord (cf. Isa. 2:3).

Ruth's Moabite identity is also discussed in the context of the period of the Judges. According to Ruth Rabbah 2:9, both she and Orpah are daughters of the Moabite king Eglon (cf. Judg. 3:12–30).[2] Some Jewish sources claimed, furthermore, that Eglon was the son of Balak, the Moabite king who asked the prophet Balaam to curse the Israelites as they approached the Promised Land (Num. 22–24). There is rabbinical discussion, for example, as to whether Ruth and Orpah converted to Judaism before their husbands died or whether Ruth alone converted at some point before her arrival in Bethlehem. In any case, her piety led to complete integration into the national storyline. According to the Talmud (Sanhedrin 93b), not only is King David her descendant, so are Daniel, Hananiah, Mishael, and Azariah—four Israelites in Babylonian exile (Dan. 1:6), as well as the future Messiah. These identifications are evidence for the practice of connecting scriptural characters in the larger scriptural storyline. The scriptural world was understood by the rabbis as an intricate whole, a meta-narrative of sorts, and they made connections of various kinds between texts and characters in the HB.

In rabbinic tradition, Orpah's fate turns badly when Naomi and Ruth depart for Bethlehem. She becomes sexually promiscuous and eventually gives birth to Goliath, the Philistine giant whom David kills (cf. 1 Sam. 17; RR 2:20; Ruth Zuta 1). In these details, she is the foil or contrast to Ruth, even as her character is filled out with this additional scriptural connection.

And what about Boaz? The Babylonian Talmud (Baba Batra 91a) and the Targum of Ruth (1:1) identify him with Ibzan of Bethlehem, one of the minor judges who had thirty sons and thirty daughters, some of whom married outside of the clan (Judg. 12:8–10). This identification connects Boaz more firmly to the period of the Judges, analogously to the depiction of Ruth as Eglon's daughter. Boaz's children and wives, and his possible age at the time of marriage to Ruth, are fascinating discussions in the sources! One tradition is that his wife died the day that Naomi and Ruth arrived from Moab (RR 3:5). He is reckoned as eighty years of age and Ruth as forty at the time of their marriage (RR 4:4, 7:4). Another tradition has him dying the day after his marriage to Ruth (Ruth Zuta 4:13).

And there is one more figure to note in this context, found in the genealogy of Jesus in Matthew's Gospel (1:5). Boaz's mother is named Rahab. Almost certainly this is the Rahab of Joshua 2, the prostitute in Jericho who assists the Israelite spies and who subsequently lived in Israel (Josh. 6:22–25). Surviving Jewish traditions do not preserve this Jewish-Christian tradition contained in Matthew 1:5. In Rabbinic sources, Rahab converts and marries Joshua (BT Megillah 14b; Ecclesiastes Rabbah 8:10).

The Place of Ruth in Canonical Collections

The rabbis and other premodern interpreters discussed the place of Ruth among the other books/scrolls of the scriptural canon. Before the invention of the printing press and subsequent fixed orders, Ruth was connected to a variety of books in canonical lists. The book's placement is an indication of how it was interpreted as part of the scriptural collection. We'll note several examples briefly. The Talmud preserves a tradition that the book comes before the Psalms (Baba Bathra 14b). The reason given is that David, the presumed writer of the Psalms, "refreshed" the Lord with his compositions. The Hebrew verb for "refresh" (*rawah*) is a play on the name *rut*. What the two books have in common—David—is the probable reason to link them and the wordplay is a secondary explanation.

For some Jewish and Christian interpreters, Ruth was counted as an appendix of Judges—that is, Judges and Ruth together were counted as one book for numbering purposes. Something similar happened with the books of Jeremiah and Lamentations. The fact that Ruth follows Judges in modern versions of the Bible thus has ancient roots. Augustine (d. 430 CE), who knew the practice of placing Ruth with Judges, commented that he thought the book should be attached to the books of Samuel which follow it (*Christian Doctrine* 2.8.13). This comment suggests that Augustine read the narrative as God's providential preparing for the rise of David as Israel's king.

Among some Syriac-speaking Christians we have evidence (Florence Codex) that they placed Ruth with the books of Esther, Judith, and Susanna to form a subcollection of narratives about holy women. Judith and Susanna are books in the Old Testament Apocrypha. A medieval Jewish tradition in the Midrash Lakach Tov points out that Ruth follows the book of Proverbs in some orders. That connection is explained in the correspondence of the "wife of substance" in Proverbs 31:10–31 (the conclusion to the book) with of Ruth, whom Boaz affirmed was a "woman of substance" (3:11). These examples illustrate the role of gender identification in the premodern period and its influence on the interpretation of Ruth.

Each of these examples illustrates the act of reading the book of Ruth in the context of the broader scriptural collections of Judaism and Christianity. Whereas the stories of Abraham and Sarah in Genesis occur at the beginning of the Pentateuch, a narrative like Ruth could be placed in more than one order to provide a broader context in which to interpret it.

These examples also show that interpreting a narrative account is something of an intertextual performance. That is one function of a scriptural collection—to provide connections between texts, as well as an orienting framework for their interpretation. In the introduction, we suggested that reading stories in the HB is like comparing and contrasting siblings. Thus, the narrator of Ruth draws on the ancestral stories in Genesis and the rise of the family of David to kingship in Israel. Later Jewish and Christian writers drew on Ruth as they extended the storyline of God's work in the world. Abraham and Sarah similarly became characters to draw upon for later instruction and reflection (Exod. 2:24; Isa. 51:2; Ps. 105:7-11; Gal. 4:21-31; Heb. 11:8-12).

SOME CHARACTERISTICS OF MODERN AND POST-MODERN RECEPTION HISTORY

Current readers of biblical narratives, who stand in the traditions of Judaism, Christianity, and Islam, can certainly apply a variety of approaches in a reading strategy. Those who investigate the influence of the narratives on the classical sources of Western society such as English or French literature and painting will pay particular attention to their reception. And there are those who read them using modern literary and philosophical methods, apart from a religious tradition or interests. Readers can share a variety of contexts and approaches! One can cite an incredibly broad range of current hermeneutical approaches, some heavily buttressed with theory and employing specialized terminology. We have said very little about them, but they are part and parcel of modern cultures. This makes them part of the world in front of a text through which current readers engage ancient texts. There are, for example, postcolonial, feminist, poststructural, and LGBTQI approaches, among many others. Perhaps the proverbial claim that "beauty is in the eye of the beholder" has cogency in every culture, but it aptly describes the massive diversity in current reading strategies and the philosophical bases for them. There are so many of them—new, modern, and traditional—that the dynamic mix marks what many call a postmodern world, with competing interests constantly under review and reformulation. As noted earlier, to introduce all these approaches, much less explore them, requires another book.[3] It is important, nevertheless, to think self-consciously about the current historical-cultural context and how it shapes the engaging of a text, ancient or otherwise.

The beginning of the chapter contained a quote from Eunny Lee, a scholar who made the point that dialogue is fundamental to the development of human identity. We then suggested that narratives in the HB are part of a dialogue from ancient Israel about its identity before God, and that readers can engage these same texts dialogically through the medium of their own experience. One of the values of reception history in biblical interpretation is its reminder that all readers of texts come to that task with prior assumptions and interests, and that dialogue with others is an important way that prior commitments are sharpened or changed. A second brief quote from Lee offers a glimpse into the shapers of meaning in the (post-) modern world. In commenting on the preponderance of dialogue in the book of Ruth, she writes: "These dialogues become an ideal vehicle for the deconstruction and reconstruction of identity and otherness."[4]

Fundamental to a modern, Western approach to life is the recognition of difference in human communities and a reticence concerning (for some a suspicion and even rejection of) a meta-narrative or universal application of a truth claim. Difference goes hand in hand with a pronounced individualism. Thus, for some, a reading strategy characterized as "deconstruction" looks for signs of fragmentation and incoherence in a narrative in order to deny its authority as a final or uniform interpretation of reality. What Lee describes as "otherness" is essentially a deeply rooted value of difference from that of an imposed uniformity in human identity. A postcolonial reading, for example, seeks to strip away or expose in literature what colonizers or those of a dominant culture impose on population groups and to recognize suppressed identities among the latter. A LGBTQI reading seeks to strip away or expose heterosexism and its assumptions, and to recognize the identities of nonheterosexuals. These are all lenses (facets of a diamond) currently existing in the world in front of a text, and they impact reading and responding to it.

THE DIVIDE AND THE BRIDGE BETWEEN THE PAST AND THE PRESENT

We have made the point repeatedly that the narratives of the HB/OT were composed and preserved to explain Israelite identity in a world created by God and to persuade their intended audiences of the cogency of that identity and ways they might respond in their time to it. The intended audiences were not only ancient, non-Western, pre-industrial communities— thus separating them variously from current readers— but also addressed corporately by these texts as a part of a transgenerational community. Primary identity resides in the people as a whole in their historical journey. Individuals and individual generations, therefore, were called to find their identity and purpose collectively as heirs of these stories. Modern individualism stands at a considerable distance from this corporate, transgenerational perspective, whether or not there might be shared religious convictions between ancient text and current readers.

We compared the narratives also to classic literature— texts from the past that are foundational for a society or culture. For many readers in Western societies, these stories are foundational for understanding that heritage and the past that gave it birth, but like the classical narratives in the *Iliad*, they are less important for current religious identity and contemporary societal values. The divide between the biblical past and Western societies is so broad that no bridge is feasible or wanted. Indifference toward a society's classics or religious heritage is one thing. The pace of modernity has deepened the divide between a religious heritage and current values across much of the globe. Hostility toward a heritage for its otherness, its rootedness in practices no longer acceptable (e.g., slavery), is increasing and something to be deplored.

And then there are modern Jews and Christians, for whom these ancient narratives are heritage and still capable of offering relevant perspectives for the responsible life of faith and human flourishing. They may not read the stories about Abraham and Sarah, or Ruth and Boaz, as confirmation of best practices for securing an heir, but they may find in them some perspectives on faith, trust, and communal commitments, which can undergird any generation of readers.

NOTES

Introduction

1. Adele Berlin, "Literary Approaches to Biblical Literature: General Observations and a Case Study in Gen 34," in *The Hebrew Bible: New Insights and Scholarship*, ed. Frederick E. Greenspahn (New York: New York University Press, 2014), 46.
2. A phrase used by the Roman orator Cicero in his *On the Laws* (1.5).
3. See further the comments in chapter 11, this volume.

Chapter 1

1. On Shalmaneser's Annals, see further comments in chapters 7 and 10, this volume.
2. On Gen. 2–3, see chapter 9, this volume.

Chapter 3

1. See chapter 8, this volume.

Chapter 4

1. There is further discussion of this passage in chapter 6, this volume.
2. There is further discussion of the term *hayil* in chapter 6, this volume.

Chapter 5

1. The Greek version has "me" and it is followed by several modern translations. The Massoretic text has "you."
2. See further discussion on these historical references in chapters 7 and 10, this volume.

Chapter 7

1. See chapter 10, this volume.
2. See the list of historical and cultural periods in the introduction to this book.
3. See chapter 10 for more on the Omride Dynasty and Jehu.

Chapter 9

1. See the discussion in chapter 2, this volume.
2. See the discussion in chapter 5, this volume.

Chapter 10

1. An alternate spelling of his name is Jehoram. Cf. 2 Kings 3:1, 6.
2. See discussion in chapter 7, this volume.

Chapter 11

1. Eunny P. Lee, "Ruth the Moabite. Identity, Kinship, and Otherness," in *Engaging the Bible in a Gendered World: An Introduction to Feminist Biblical Interpretation in Honor of Katharine Doob Sakenfeld*, ed. Linda Day and Carolyn Pressler (Louisville: Westminster John Knox Press, 2006), 93.
2. For discussion of Eglon and the period of the Judges, see chapter 7, this volume.
3. See Dana Nolan Fewell, ed., *The Oxford Handbook of Biblical Narrative* (Oxford: Oxford University Press, 2016).
4. Lee, "Ruth the Moabite," p. 93.

BIBLIOGRAPHY

Alter, Robert. 1981. *The Art of Biblical Narrative.* New York: Basic Books.

Amit, Yaira. 2000. *Hidden Polemics in Biblical Narrative.* Leiden: Brill.

Arnold, Bill T., and H. G. M. Williamson, eds. 2005. *Dictionary of the Old Testament: Historical Books.* Downers Grove, IL: InterVarsity Press.

Arnold, Bill T., and Richard S. Hess, eds. 2014. *Ancient Israel's History: An Introduction to Issues and Sources.* Grand Rapids, MI: Eerdmans.

Auld, A. Graeme. 2017. *Life in Kings: Reshaping the Royal Story in the Hebrew Bible.* Atlanta, GA: Society of Biblical Literature.

Bar-Efrat, Shimon. 2004. *Narrative Art in the Bible.* London: Bloomsbury.

Becking, Bob, and Susan Hennecke, eds. 2010. *Out of Paradise: Eve and Adam and their Interpreters.* Sheffield: Phoenix Press.

Berlin, Adele. 1983. *Poetics and Interpretation of Biblical Narrative.* Sheffield: Almond Press.

Berlin, Adele. 2014. "Literary Approaches to Biblical Literature: General Observations and a Case Study in Gen 34." In *The Hebrew Bible: New Insights and Scholarship*, edited by Frederick E. Greenspahn, 45–75. New York: New York University Press.

Billings, Rachel M. 2013. *"Israel Served the Lord": The Book of Joshua as Paradoxical Portrait of Faithful Israel*. Notre Dame, IN: University of Notre Dame Press.

Blenkinsopp, Joseph. 2015. *Abraham: The Story of a Life*. Grand Rapids, MI: Eerdmans.

Borgen, Paul. 2008. *David, Saul, and God: Rediscovering an Ancient Story*. Oxford: Oxford University Press.

Brown, William P. 2017. *A Handbook to Old Testament Exegesis*. Louisville, KY: Westminster John Knox Press.

Carr, David M. 2005. *Writing on the Tablet of the Heart: Origins of Scripture and Literature*. Oxford: Oxford University Press.

Carvalho, Corrine L. 2009. *Primer on Biblical Methods*. Winona, MN: Liturgical Press.

Caspi, Mishael M., and John T. Greene, eds. 2012. *Portraits of a King Favored by God: David the King: God's Poet, Warrior, and Statesman*. Piscataway, NJ: Gorgias Press.

Chalmers, Aaron. 2013. *Exploring the Religion of Ancient Israel: Priest, Prophet, Sage and People*. Downers Grove, IL: InterVarsity Press.

Clines, D. J. A. 1997. *The Theme of the Pentateuch*. 2nd ed. London: A & C Black.

de Jong, I. J. F., R. Nünlist, and A. Bowie. 2004. *Narrators, Narratees and Narratives in Ancient Greek Literature*. Leiden: Brill.

Dozeman, Thomas B. 2017. *The Pentateuch: Introducing the Torah*. Philadelphia, PA: Fortress Press.

Dozeman, Thomas B., Konrad Schmid, and Thomas Römer, eds. 2011. *Pentateuch, Hexateuch, or Enneateuch: Identifying Literary Works in Genesis through Kings*. Atlanta, GA: Society of Biblical Literature.

Dutcher-Walls, Patricia. 2014. *Reading the Historical Books: A Student's Guide to Engaging the Biblical Text*. Grand Rapids, MI: Baker.

Fewell, Dana Nolan, ed. 2016. *The Oxford Handbook of Biblical Narrative*. Oxford: Oxford University Press.

Fleming, Daniel E. 2009. "The Heavens Were Not Enough: Humanity and God's Home in the Book of Genesis." In *Reconstructing a Distant Past: Ancient Near Eastern Essays in Tribute to Jorge R. Silva Castillo*, edited by D. A. Barrevra Fracaroli and G. del Olmo Lete, 103–105. Barcelona: Editorial AUSA.

Frankel, David. 2011. *The Land of Canaan and the Destiny of Israel: Theologies of Territory in the Hebrew Bible.* Winona Lake, IN: Eisenbrauns.

Freedman, Amelia D. 2005. *God as an Absent Character in biblical Hebrew Narrative: A Literary-theoretical Study.* New York: Peter Lang.

Galvin, Garrett. 2016. *David's Successors: Kingship in the Old Testament.* Winona, MN: Liturgical Press.

Gravett, Sandra L., Karla G. Bohmback, F. V. Greifenhagen, and Donald C. Polaski. 2008. *An Introduction to the Hebrew Bible: A Thematic Approach.* Louisville, KY: Westminster John Knox Press.

Gregg, Robert C. 2015. *Shared Stories, Rival Tellings: Early Encounters of Jews, Christians, and Muslims.* New York: Oxford University Press.

Gunn, David M. 1978. *The Story of King David: Genre and Interpretation.* JSOTSS 6. Sheffield: Sheffield Academic Press.

Hallo, William W., and K. Lawson Younger, eds. 1997, 2000, 2002. *The Context of Scripture.* 3 vols. Leiden: Brill.

Hawk, L. Daniel. 2012. "The Truth about Conquest: Joshua as History, Narrative, and Scripture." *Interpretation* 66: 129–40.

Hawkins, Ralph. 2013. *How Israel Became a People.* Nashville, TN: Abingdon Press.

Holm, Tawny L. 2013. Of Courtiers and Kings. *The Biblical Daniel Narratives and Ancient Story-Collections.* Winona Lake, IN: Eisenbrauns.

Hornsby Teresa J., and Deryn Guest. 2016. *Transgender, Intersex, and Biblical Interpretation.* Atlanta, GA: Society of Biblical Literature.

King, Philip J., and Lawrence E. Stager. 2002. *Life in Biblical Israel.* Louisville, KY: Westminster John Knox Press.

Koosed, Jennifer L. 2011. *Gleaning Ruth: A Biblical Heroine and Her Afterlives.* Columbia: University of South Carolina Press.

Kratz, Reinhard G. 2005. *The Composition of the Narrative Books of the Old Testament.* New York: T & T Clark.

Lamb, David T. 2015. *Prostitutes and Polygamists: A Look at Love, Old Testament Style.* Grand Rapids, MI: Zondervan.

Lau, Peter Hon Wan. 2010. *Identity and Ethics in the Book of Ruth: A Social Identity Approach.* Berlin: de Gruyter.

Lee, Eunny P. 2006. "Ruth the Moabite: Identity, Kinship, and Otherness." In *Engaging the Bible in a Gendered World: An Introduction to Feminist Biblical Interpretation in Honor of Katharine Doob Sakenfeld*, edited by Linda Day and Carolyn Pressler, 89–101. Louisville, KY: Westminster John Knox Press.

Leuchter, Mark. 2013. *Samuel and the Shaping of Tradition.* Oxford: Oxford University Press.

Leuchter, Mark A., and David T. Lamb. 2016. *The Historical Writings: Introducing Israel's Historical Literature.* Minneapolis, MN: Fortress Press.

Lieb, Michael, Emma Mason, Jonathan Roberts, and Christopher Rowland, eds. 2011. *The Oxford Handbook on the Reception History of the Bible.* Oxford: Oxford University Press.

Lynch, Matthew. 2014. *Monotheism and Institutions in the Book of Chronicles: Temple, Priesthood, and Kingship in Post-exilic Perspective.* Tübingen: Mohr Siebeck.

Marais, Jacobus. 1998. *Representation in Old Testament Narrative Texts.* Leiden: Brill.

McConville, J. Gordon. 2016. *Being Human in God's World: An Old Testament Theology of Humanity.* Grand Rapids, MI: Baker Academic.

McLaughlin, John L. 2017. *What Are They Saying About Ancient Israelite Religion?* Mahwah, NJ: Paulist Press.

Meyers, Carol. 2012. *Rediscovering Eve: Ancient Israelite Women in Context.* Oxford: Oxford University Press.

Moffat, Donald P. 2013. *Ezra's Social Drama: Identity Formation, Marriage and Social Conflict in Ezra 9 and 10.* London: Bloomsbury.

Newsom, Carol. 2003. *The Book of Job: A Contest of Moral Imaginations.* New York: Oxford University Press.

Nielsen, Kirsten. 1997. *Ruth: A Commentary.* Louisville, KY: Westminster John Knox Press.

O'Connell, Robert H. 1995. *Rhetoric of the Book of Judges.* Leiden: Brill.

Otto, Suzanne. 2003. "The Composition of the Elijah-Elisha Stories and the Deuteronomistic History." *Journal for the Study of the Old Testament* 27: 487–508.

Person, Raymond F., and Robert Rezetko, eds. 2016. *Empirical Models Challenging Biblical Criticism.* Atlanta, GA: Society of Biblical Literature.

Polzin, Robert. 1993. *David and the Deuteronomist: 2 Samuel.* Bloomington: Indiana University Press.

Provan, Iain. 2014. *Seriously Dangerous Religion: What the Old Testament Really Says and Why It Matters.* Waco, TX: Baylor University Press.

Sakenfeld, Katharine Doob, ed. 2006. *The New Interpreters Dictionary of the Bible.* 5 vols. Nashville, TN: Abingdon.

Sasson, Jack M. 2009. "Ethically Cultured Interpretations: The Case of Eglon's Murder (Judges 3)." In *Homeland and Exile. Biblical and Ancient Near Eastern Studies in Honour of Bustenay Oded*, edited by Gershon Galil, Mark Geller, and Alan Millard, 571–96. Leiden: Brill.

Saxegaard, Kristen. 2010. *Character Complexity in the Book of Ruth.* Tübingen: Mohr Siebeck.

Schmidt, Brian B., ed. 2015. *Contextualizing Israel's Sacred Writings: Ancient Literacy, Orality, and Literary Production.* Atlanta, GA: Society of Biblical Literature.

Southwood, Katherine. 2012. *Ethnicity and Mixed Marriages in Ezra 9-10: An Anthropological Approach.* Oxford: Oxford University Press.

Sternberg, Meir. 1985. *The Poetics of Biblical Narrative: Ideological Literature and the Drama of Reading.* Bloomington: Indiana University Press.

Strawn, Brent A. 2017. *The Old Testament is Dying: A Diagnosis and Recommended Treatment.* Grand Rapids, MI: Baker Academic.

Trible, Phyllis, and Letty M. Russell, eds. 2006. *Hagar, Sarah, and Their Children: Jewish, Christian, and Muslim Perspectives.* Louisville, KY: Westminster John Knox Press.

Tull, Patricia K., and Jacqueline E. Lapsley, eds. 2015. *After Exegesis: Feminist Biblical Theology.* Waco, TX: Baylor University Press.

Vette, Joachim. 2010. "Narrative Poetics and Hebrew Narrative: A Survey." In *Literary Construction of Identity in the Ancient World*, edited by Hanna Liss and Manfred Oeming, 19–61. Winona Lake, IN: Eisenbrauns.

Walsh, Jerome T. 2001. *Style and Structure in Biblical Hebrew Narrative.* Collegeville, MN: Liturgical Press.

Webb, Barry G. 2008. *Book of Judges: An Integrated Reading*. Eugene, OR: Wipf and Stock.

Wray Beal, Lisa M. 2014. *1 & 2 Kings*. Downers Grove, IL: InterVarsity Press.

Yamasaki, Gary. 2007. *Watching a Biblical Narrative: Point of View in Biblical Exegesis*. New York: T & T Clark.

Yoo, Philip Y. 2016. "Hagar the Egyptian: Wife, Handmaid, and Concubine." *Catholic Biblical Quarterly* 78: 215–35.

INDEX OF SELECT BIBLICAL AND

QURANIC TEXTS

INDEX